cokemachine

Published in the United States by:
Archway Editions,
a division of powerHouse Cultural Entertainment, Inc.
32 Adams Street, Brooklyn, NY 11201

www.archwayeditions.us

Daniel Power, CEO
Chris Molnar, Editorial Director
Nicodemus Nicoludis, Managing Editor
Naomi Falk, Editor

Library of Congress Control Number: 2022940429

ISBN 978-1-57687-997-9

Printed by Toppan Leefung

First edition, 2022

10 9 8 7 6 5 4 3 2 1

Interior layout and design by Chris Molnar

Printed and bound in China

ARCHWAY
EDITIONS

cokemachineglow

WRITING AROUND MUSIC 2005-2015

Archway Editions, Brooklyn, NY

CONTENTS

INTRODUCTION

The writing in this collection was originally published on Cokemachineglow.com between the years 2006 and 2015. CMG had been publishing for a few years prior to this date. I joined the site in 2005, when it was already a bustling ecosystem: there was a layer of associate editors in place, a lively messageboard, a fairly involved application process involving not one but two reviews written on spec and pro bono. Everything for CMG, it's worth clarifying up front, was pro bono, up to and including this intro. Scott Reid, the site's founder and editor in chief, placed some banner ads on the site, all of which accrued approximately fuck-all, and didn't even come close to recouping the expenses of running a site, manually laying out each homepage (we didn't have a CMS until we built one, in 2008), sequencing and mixing monthly playlists, sourcing writers, managing personality clashes, editing and promoting somewhere between 4 and 12 record reviews every week, not to mention concert reviews, track reviews, blog posts, sprawling concert reviews and features and a handful of recurring columns—all in all, something like 5,732 pieces of content, including lists.

We all wrote for free, too, which is something increasingly and justifiably frowned upon in the modern media ecosystem but which is, in hindsight, sort of inextricable from the Cokemachineglow experience. We wrote for free because we had to write, and, while every now and then we mounted an effort to sell out, to turn all our effort into part-time compensation, or at least like "weed money," it's also obvious that this was a site that was not going to be tamed, which is to say become profitable: that writerly indulgence and a frankly pretty emo sense of self-flagellation was absolutely inextricable from the site's appeal, from what bound us to its mission and to each other in the first place. Our sentences were all too long, too. Cokemachineglow's house style was "too much." When it worked, it worked: free-form creative nonfiction spurred from an aesthetic reaction to the music we loved but situated deeply in the experience of being young, afloat on student loans, and probably drunk. When CMG's writing didn't work, well, it didn't, and the writer knew it. One thread on the forum titled Staff On Staff ("not as hot as it sounds," read Scott's description) served as a forum for feedback, and said feedback was really the only compensation any of us needed or wanted for our labor. There was nothing worse than going all-in on some massive, diaristic concert review and seeing that thread remain dormant afterward.

I don't want to belabor the point, but belaboring the point is sort of the point. Cokemachineglow's staff—dozens of writers, in its full timeline, but composed generally of a handful of heavy contributors fading in and out of the hivemind—wrote primarily for each other, with readers amassing in the wake. We arrived as wildly ambitious writers and left as slightly better ones, indulgences either tamed and better wrenched into the copy or enflamed and doomed forever to burst unbidden from every overstuffed sentence we create. Either way: better. Our traffic figures were Monopoly money compared to what would even seem quantifiable today, but mainstream publications noticed: We got shouted out in *Spin*, *Entertainment Weekly*, and *Newsweek*; Robert Christgau got mad at us for an Eminem review; we were a music writer's music website, passed along like a secret. Some writers went on to better things: Lindsay Zoladz was the first to decamp to *Pitchfork*, then to *New York* and the *New York Times*; Calum Marsh found his way to the *New Yorker* and the *Guardian*; Colin McGowan is that rarest of things, a professional basketball blogger; Andre Perry published an NPR-acclaimed collection of essays; Dom worked at *Paste* for a long tenure, Eric at *Buzzfeed* and *IGN*, Molnar at the publishing house that's publishing this very book, and so on. Turns out the CMG "process"—a bunch of writers, writing their asses off, attracting more writers to fill the spots left by writers who burned out or moved onto bigger things—got results. It just didn't make money.

I originally attempted to compile this collection in 2015, around the time of the site's shuttering, under the title "The Old, Weird Internet Is Dead." This felt extremely relevant at the time, when *Wondering Sound*, *The Dissolve*, and *Grantland* had all recently also shuttered, while *Pitchfork* had been recently acquired by Conde Nast, truly a case of "the pigs walking like humans," if you want to see it that way. But I don't, really. *Pitchfork* has aged nicely, in its glossy era, and, for all the heated rhetoric of the early 2000s Blog Wars, it was always a good site. It was first, for sure, inspiring a raft of likeminded webzines full of young writers delirious on the possibilities of the internet as a means to bypass the gatekeepers of print journalism. Money was beside the point for a generation who thought "a byline" was a sacred gift and now realized that, nope, bylines were free! baby and you could spend the first 250 words of your Bravery write-up bitching about hipsters. CMG, before it developed a reputation as either "the writerly music website (in a good way)" or "the writerly music website (in a bad way)," had a reputation as the Canadian one, thanks to the fact that a number of early editors were based out of the country, and because "Canadian indie rock" was a then-congealing principle (think: Arcade Fire, Feist, Wolf Parade), and because the site's name was lifted from a book of poetry by the lead singer of the beloved Canadian outfit the Tragically Hip. Anyway, we were soon stretched out in Ohio, Chicago, L.A., Iowa, Portland, London, and so on—not Canadian in any sense except the way everyone freaked out about every new Frog Eyes record.

My original attempt at a compilation dissolved when my rough draft equaled several hundred thousand words. Attempting to tell the story of a website comprehensively or even representatively (in terms of staff effort) is impossible, and anyway, we wrote a fucking lot, as you are remembering with each of these sentences (sorry). Molnar reached out to me in late 2020 to revive the project in the form you hold in your hands, and that very tactility inspired me to go narrow. I whittled down a massive list of nominees, realizing the story to tell is of the site itself: a chronological history of its editorial voice. (You can see the more comprehensive longlist on the site now, if interested.) Pieces are presented here largely, save some nips and tucks, as they were on the site. The early era is full of life: wily stuff, frequently written in the recurring form of a stage-play or Socratic dialogue, full of in-jokes and almost pubescent angst at the state of music criticism. Around the turn of the decade, the presence of a few new voices helped the site coalesce into what I think of as its most regal era, where the "personal angle" wasn't relegated to the intro but instead suffused into the fabric of the piece. And in the last few years, you see the strain it took to maintain this: writers flaming out and quitting the site mid-article, the encroachment of age and irrelevance, an awareness of the site's homogeneity and permanent-underdog status and the increasingly overheated temperature of online discourse as the oblivion of 2015 approached. You can read the story of the old, weird internet in these pages.

But I got the title wrong, on that first draft: It isn't dead. When Molnar approached me to revive this project, he said he still wondered, flatly put, What did it all mean? What did all that effort amount to? You can map the editorial voice of the site evolving alongside Twitter, and its corresponding feel of permanently self-immolating critical groupthink. CMG raged against this, and the CMG Twitter account, which is still running, still occasionally issues trollish jabs at the machine. But CMG's glory days were not about its puckish contrarianism. It was about the life of its writers and the interplay between them. Two of our most long-standing editorial formats were the Counterpoint—in which a writer respectfully but fully disagreed with the scored review of another writer—and the Collaboration—in which multiple writers wrote over and around and between each other to more fully express a shared experience of a piece of music. There is a reason why, again and again, we returned to reviews in the form of written dialogues. We were finding our voices in the context of each other. What attracted readers to Cokemachineglow was the sense of community that radiated off of the work, the way Nool and Betz and Boogz were recurring characters within the pieces, how you saw writers strive mightily, hit a dry spell, taper off, and then emerge to knock one out of the park.

CMG didn't die because the internet no longer had a place for it; it died because we aged out of doing this shit for free. But the spirit of the old, weird internet lives on: it exists in the curated communities under Substack posts, in Letterboxd and Goodreads, on private Discords; it exists on TikTok and Twitch and whatever else I'm probably too old to know about, wherever people with a surplus of free time and creativity are goading each other to delirious new heights; it exists in longform YouTube exegeses and strikingly sincere "reacts" videos. Of course, these are all corporate platforms, designed around such social interactions, and monetized to profit off of free labor. But maybe it's helpful to think of Cokemachineglow as a platform, a Web 2.0 Blogspot-era product with the germs of the full social era laying dormant inside. The internet was always going to become the thing it has become. The writing contained within this collection shows one way in which that used to be expressed: longform music criticism, written not as some professional endeavor but because it had to be written, because it was the expression of a community full of people—and this is worth being clear about—that just really, really liked music. If there is something that this collection makes me miss, it's that: the thrill of poring over new music and diving so deeply into it that you emerge like a crazed acolyte, charting its metaphors on a pinboard and weaving its waveforms into your daily life, seeing art not as a two-dimensional or even score-able thing but an ongoing and enduring part of the way that we do the things that we do. This relationship has grown more rare, in the years since CMG's inception and even its demise: the platforms, again, have had their say, and music is constant, free, etc.—almost a source of passive identification rather than a direct one. In that sense alone, perhaps this book can serve as a reminder. The writing glows, still, with the joy of discovery.

DESTROYER: DESTROYER'S RUBIES (COUNTERPOINT)

Aaron Newell
10 March 2006

My Mom once cried when she caught me watching the video to the Roots' "What They Do." Notice I say "caught," for context, since in most families the watching of music videos is not prohibited under penalty of weeping-parent guilt trip. I was busy minding my own business, laughing at the video-dancer's butt-cramp. Mom, however, mistook my laughter for the lustful manic cackles of a virile and virally insatiable testosteroned boner-bound teenage male. Truth is I was drunk and waiting for some friends to come over so I could continue getting drunk, except in the woods. At this precise moment, with furry-stars aligned, the video bordered on funny—worthy of a giggle, surely. But Mom cried because she figured rap music + bikini-babe + butt + chuckles = she failed as mother, son obviously a sexual deviant. All she really needed to do was keep track of Dad's beer in the fridge and the problem would have solved itself.

Once, on my way to a tennis lesson, I was playing Milli Vanilli's album (Fab R.I.P.) (or, maybe, Rob R.I.P., sorry guys) and the song "All or Nothing" came on. This song featured the line "All or Nothing / What's it gonna be / Something's gotta show / When you're lying under me." After years of scrutiny, I have determined that this song is about a man who does not like it when a girl with whom he is undergoing a period of courting refuses to fornicate with him. He finds this inconvenient, perhaps frustrating, almost to the point where he threatens to jeopardize the entire relationship by breaking up with her, and thereby being forced to return her dowry. In an unappreciated act of behavioural music criticism, Mom threw my tape out of the car window. In an unappreciated act of fitting, karmic music criticism, the cassette died under the wheel of a tailgating Renault Le Car with no muffler.

My inner (still kidding myself) music nerd has had some struggles to this point, you could say. I couldn't very well explain the Public Enemy bomber jacket or the *Sex And Violence* (1992) cover art. I never played Mariah Carey for fear of my mind being read. Still, there have been times when I've done well with pärentmœzik, just once, with My Morning Jacket's *It Still Moves* (2003), only. I thought Iron & Wine would be safe until Sam Beam finally sang something remotely smutty on *Woman King* (2005) with his "We were born to fuck each other one way or another" line. I had just e-mailed the album to Dad as "dinner music." Roughly 21 minutes and 13 seconds later I called him up, anxiously stammering over my intended words "DON'T PLAY TRACK SIX WE WILL NEVER BE ABLE TO LISTEN TO MUSIC AGAIN" when he pre-empted my expressed concern, answering the phone with a meek "Too late." In the background I could hear the acetic sound of tissues being pulled, and sniffles, and a CDR, cutting through the tension in the air, on its way out the window.

There is obviously a generation gap prevalent in my very musically inclined family. And for all of my mother's memorizing the lyrics to each vittle of Rod Stewart's early work, and for all of the pictures of Bruce Springsteen's butt that decorate my family's record collection, and especially for all of the times that listening to Dire Straits also meant that Knopfler's millionaire "faggot" was to be explained away as "a cigarette, in old English" ("But Dad, how does a cigarette earn money?" I would ask, fearlessly dismantling Freud even as an 8-year-old), I still got brung-up-proper for rapping-too-loud-in-the-mirror to A Tribe Called Quest's "What?" ("What is a poet? / All balls / No cock"). I could not pass this off as Q-Tip's invocation of Chicken George's plight as a cockfighter as portrayed by significant African American writer Alex Haley in his historically valuable and canonical literary work *Roots* (1976), despite my best efforts. Invocations of Steve Biko and USC open mic nights also fell on deaf ears.

I've moved out, recently. I can now listen to what I want, in open air, except when I'm on the phone to my parents, or someone they may know, or when they're thinking about me. I've been using this new freedom to explore my own tendencies—poking my head out from under the umbrella of punitive scorn, and discovering a few things about being a kid. One thing I've realized is that it's important not to give up on your favorite bad words if there's a little something more to them than shock value. Given the right circumstances and presentation, even the most sensitive of parental constitutions might allow for some parental advisory-style content. This, if you couldn't tell, is one such story.

To set the stage a little more (and please don't get the impression that I'm 19, it's much worse than that): if I was 19, and played for my parents an album that contained such muddy obloquy as "She needs release, she needs to feel at peace with her father, the fucking maniac," and "Why didn't we stop fucking around, you girls like gazelles, raise boys wearing bells, blaze new trails in the South," and "Hey your friends are fucked insofar as your friends are an ancient beast," it would have been strictly The Safe Sounds Of Catholicism: Christmastime! all year round, and maybe Zamfir on weekends, forever.

This past holiday season was different, however. I visited my folks for three weeks, staying in a room with a stereo that could not push "1" on the volume dial without the rattling of the speakers drowning out the music supposedly emitted therefrom. The town being "comatose" at its most caffeinated, the local radio station, singular, wasn't always cranking out Baltimore Club, and while some of the stuff it played sounded like Cat Power's new stuff, it wasn't. This left me with few opportunities for new music intake. We did, however, have sightseeing to do. This meant long drives, which meant a required amount of respite from the radio. David Gray was safe. The communal My Morning Jacket, Sam Beam pre-*Woman King*, and M. Ward CDs were all almost see-through from overplay. It's impossible to enjoy the Afro Cuban All-Stars when it's cloudy, and that just about did it for the agreeable parts of Dad's collection. My thoughts about my own CD wallet included "Well, *We Got it For Cheap Vol. II* (2005) has some well-known beats on it" and "I wonder if, to a Billy Joel fan, Spencer Krug or Thom Yorke has a more conventional voice."

My mail was being forwarded from home. *Destroyer's Rubies* (2006) showed up, after I begged for it. A literate, sometimes-traditional-rock-based Canadian connoisseur of drinking alcoholic things fit the loaded family sedan better than the Re-Up Gang. In anticipation of Rubies, and the possibility of reviewing it or writing a 6-page blog entry that mentioned it, I had recently purchased everything else in the Destroyer catalogue, omitting his first-ever recording *We'll Build Them a Golden Bridge* (1996), not quite ready to look up the man's skirt just yet. I was, however, ready for sparse folk-rock and choked yelps (*Thief* [2000], *City Of Daughters* [1998]), and possibly some cheesy midi synth overglaze (*Your Blues* [2004]), and hopefully borderline pub-rock that featured huge, sometimes impromptu, sparkling guitar solos (*Streethawk* [2001], *This Night* [2002]), and definitely clay-ball lyrics that could arguably be on the subject of either 1) past lovers, or 2) the music industry, or 3) popular perception of music as art, or 4) Destroyer, or 5) all four, at the same time, or 6) absolutely nothing at all, depending on how my day was going before listening.

Dad and I were both desperate for some possibly suitable new music. We cracked open my mail, and our family outing was being soundtracked by Bejar before I could say "lyric sheet."

Now, it's time for some CMG context. Chet reviewed *Rubies* for us. Scott asked me to, and boy did I want to, but I balked, sort of choked, because there's a shitload of people out there writing about Bejar, inventing drinking games in his honour, interpreting his words, generally being annoying shits about it. This is no different. Probably it's worse. It took me about two weeks to decide how to write about this album, and then, once I had finally settled on the least-bad idea—tough decision, tight race—my laptop crashed, kind of like, "I want no part of this." But Scott feels like I do about this record, has the same dedication to it, which doesn't happen too often, and therefore suggested that I do a counterpoint, because "It's just wrong to have this album rated so low." So while we officially have 73 as our "grade" for *Rubies*, average that out with something like a 92. I like Chet a lot, he's a great, tolerant guy, can explain Wolf Parade, looks good as a zombie, etc., but Cokemachineglow not signifying that this album is something that will be adored by those precious people who love music so much that they hate 95% of it, well, that makes me pissy and spiteful.

Which are words that I cannot use in front of my parents. Even "spite," as it falls under my Mom's list of supplementary deadly sins.

Ever try to fake being asleep, but you can't, because you're flinching and going "UH" and "GA" involuntarily because one of your favorite songwriters is cussing his curly hair straight while your folks digest every word of it? Or perhaps you're a daring, proactive devil child, tensely anticipating the word "fuck" with more precision than a Super Bowl half-time broadcast delay, blurting things like "HEYTHERELOOKATTHEPRICEOFGASATTHATPLACE BOYDOESWARSTINK" seconds too late. Or have you ever faked choking on nothing? These are all ineffective, embarrassingly obvious tactics for drowning out a cursing stereo from the back seat of a car.

Now, I generally try to reserve turning blue for special occasions like getting dunked in a swimming pool or singing along with Emperor X. If I can avoid bursting blood vessels in my eyes, I will do so. But I will hack and wheeze on purpose if it will save me from getting thrown out of the sunroof. Imagine, then, my mixed and conflicted feelings, my own emotional Gwen Stefani outfit of disappointment and astonishment when, despite Bejar belting out baddies in a song called "European Oils" of all things, my mother, Puritan Pop Priestess, She Who Believes That Rod Stewart Was All About The Cuddling, was listening intently, interestedly, calmly, her personal censorship sensories napping through "She needs relief, she needs to feel at peace with her father—the fucking maniac," and I was thankfully not ejected from the car, under the wheels of a dying Renault, or, worse, disowned, as that would have been very embarrassing for a twenty-something during Christmas, with my girlfriend in the seat next to me.

Who, incidentally, being fully aware of how special it was for me not to be parentally divorced on the spot at this time, did a really cute "wow" thing with her eyebrows right after Bejar sullied our earholes.

And things remained calm, serene even, idle chit-chat filling the gaps between songs, the entire car hushing promptly with each melodic hint at another fresh, furtive carol. Danny's nimble, sailing guitar solos and plaintive organ complements and twinkling keys and soothesaid abstractions seemed as breathlessly anticipated by my priggish progenitors as his "Shadowy figures babbling on about typical rural shit" and "Pure shit from which nothing ever rose" and, of course, his fucked friends as ancient beasts + fucked girls like gazelles. I began to daydream suitable conversations that might follow the *Rubies* listening: "Aaron, where is this talented young lady from?" "He's from British Columbia, Mom, where I get all that pot—wanna buy some?" "Yes, how kind!" I bailed on that, of course, choosing to push my luck in other domains: we made it through the entire album twice (in Argos voice).

Now, I have my theories on how this was possible. And the fact that I'm here to tell this story is proof that Mr. Betz is wrong in his estimation of *Destroyer's Rubies* when he wicks on about "frustration" at "heft" and "pomposity" and "the emptiness" of Bejar's semantic-less la's on "Rubies" and "European Oils" and "Looters' Follies" and "A Dangerous Woman" and "Priest's Knees" and "on and on" and "73%." Complaining that "There's no words to this Destroyer chorus!" is the equivalent of chastising a soloing guitar for not having teeth and a tongue, or asking James Brown to elocute in iambic pentameter. No one can sing a wink like Dan Bejar, and just as Spencer Krug can sing "la" and convey the guilt in an entire generation's gluttony, and Kelis can sing "la" and cause a physiological reaction, and Colin Meloy can sing "la" and convey what's inside a wasted mind's desire for a decent glass of shiraz, and Ashlee Simpson can sing "la" and convey "bone" (verb), and the Delfonics will spell it out and say it means "I love you," so can Bejar use the context of his song to cause the listener to wonder about how his room at the castle paid for itself on "Rubies," or to poke fun at his character's own bar-leaning lament on "European Oils," or to convey a chorus of the good 'ol boys supporting one of their own as he spins off a drunk rant on "Looter's Follies," or to convey the extent of his carefree escapism on "Priest's Knees," or to convey the absolute nothingness of grandiose "life" statements—especially those sung by Michael Stipe—on "Watercolours Into The Ocean," which is arguably about the dilution of popular music in the greater cumulative pool of successive eras of popular art, and how almost everything eventually bleeds together anyway, despite the confluence of unique voices in any one era, until all you get is one big wet blanket statement that's made up of parts indistinguishable one from the other (like, for example, how "la's" look on paper), which, in turn, encourages the listener to wring each piece of art for all it's worth before it melts away into the abyss, like, I dunno, a tall ship made of snow, invading the sun, maybe.

I'm quite satisfied with "la." Especially when "la" is accompanied by a rejuvenated Neil Young "Down By The River" guitar lick ("Sick Priest"), or when sung in road-worn Beatles harmonies, or complemented with beautifully fleshed-out, but rough-edged, pub-rock instrumentation not unlike Rod's better years ("Your Blood"), or when featuring shimmering soloed guitar work that might remind one's folks of their favorite Dire Straits moments, all smeared over with a ratpack swagger sung through the nose, and as if that would cause severe tension and irritability, which the vocalist would barely be just not slick enough to conceal. In that context, "la" works. As do the "f" and "s" words, because, surrounded and sung by intriguing characters in songs that feature ancient, beautifully structured melodies that struggle out from the back of the mass consciousness's mind, the potential for offense disappears under the pleasantness of nostalgia. And Bejar sells this, repackaged with a gloss of eccentric abstraction, decorated with tangential jam sequences, multiple refrains scattered throughout each track, and enough consistency in symbol and imagery to persuade the poetry seekers that there's a coherent theme to be divined. He's the difference between a used car salesman and a dealer of refurbished antiques.

Now, as is evidenced by the foregoing shitty list of comparisons—and please note that I'm not limiting the album to any particular touchstones, I'm just suggesting that it has a "back then" feel, overall—*Destroyer's Rubies* evinces an awareness of a feeling that "I've heard something like this before, and really enjoyed it" while denying the listener enough material specifics to follow-up with "It was on this record, recorded by this band, which I listened to when I was this old" (unless, of course, you sit down and think about that for two weeks…). *Rubies* conjures AM fuzz and plays with fuzzy memory. And that's the fun, but it's also a comment on the canon it invokes. Bejar's arrangements highlight how disparate elements of rock "history" can easily bleed into each other when faced with a pop go-forward basis, and how there's always a little stale in every fresh sound, which is full-on Arts Degree cliché, given. But the record differentiates itself by flirting with the dark side of the "culture soundtrack," straddling that line, drawing attention to the deep, dry rut on its other side. The charm is that it avoids falling in by keeping the rut as pretty as possible through gorgeous melody, playful instrumentation, humble bluster, all tricks learned in that very same trench. And this still wouldn't be enough if it weren't for Bejar's perpetual wink, his continuous recall of certain symbols and lines, his own personal set of pens-that-look-like-swords-that-look-like-cigars. He juggles them all, always in total control, never stabbing, slicing, or burning himself, and telling us all about it as he's going, and moving on: "…but leave I must, as gratifying as this dust was…" ("Rubies"). Of course that's a reference to a record jacket, I'm sure of it. —

To further wit: "Watercolours Into The Ocean," the voice of which leads by example with these lines: "Listening to Strawberry Wine for the 131st time / It was 1987 / It was Spring / Now it's 1987 all the time." This is Deana Carter's "Strawberry Wine," right? Of course not, it's Pat Benatar's. Or, more likely, The Band. Or My Bloody Valentine's *Strawberry Wine* EP (1987). Definitely not Ryan Adams, hopefully. Regardless, if you let this verse be as figurative as it wants to be, you come to the conclusion that it's all of the above, and then some, forever. On *Rubies*, a "song" is not a specific set of words and notes and voices and instruments conveying them, a song is a melting pot of all that's come before it, and a foreshadow of what's coming next. Bejar's reference to the multifaceted words "Strawberry Wine," with or without italics, dares the listener to pick an influence from the pot, and proceed from there, stuck to an assigned connotation (which is the precise moment that it becomes "1987 all the time…"). For all we know, the voice in the song is drunk on a bottle of the "literal" stuff, out of habit, for the nth time, and following its voices down memory lane. But that's not as fun as playing fish-for-your-favorite-band, which is the game that each of the songs on *Rubies* begs the listener to play, once "Watercolours Into The Ocean" drops the hint.

The stimulus of all classic rock, all at once, might translate simply into "Bowie" for Bowie enthusiasts (which is Bejar's sideshow tent, no doubt), but here's a different spin: *Rubies* sounds like a classic rock album not only by sounding like a lot of classic rock albums, but by sounding like them all, all at once, without giving up any one single ghost. The trick lies in the carefully carved rough edges, the melodies and harmonies that recall past favorites, but that never supplant their voices for its own, keeping the curtain pulled tight across the '60s and '70s, letting in enough light to tease with silhouettes only (see if you can spot the outline of Elton John's giant, starry-eyed sunglasses). And that's a great trick. And yeah the record sprawls and gets actively disorganized in parts, and yeah it's a big, ugly hat made of all the other hats that Bejar has tried on, but hey, Chet, that's a new hat too, right? If you want to discuss self-parody through headwear then I'll talk Busta Rhymes with you any day. But I don't see it here. Bejar references himself as much as other songwriters—in lyrics and arrangement and delivery and melody alike, maybe both consciously and not, depending on the lick. But instead of numbering the dots, he just dumps them onto the paper, leaving us to find a discernible form. I'm not trying to mix metaphors, but Scott calls it "writing in inkblots," and we all know what those are used for. But try turning it around sometime, ask, "I wonder what these say about old Rorschach?" You ever think he was tempted to sign one of those things? Call it a Pollock? Anyone can throw paint on a canvas, explain the hell out of it later, or maybe even leave that to someone else, right? You still have to pick your colors first, no matter what.

So this Christmas, in the middle of *Destroyer's Rubies'* car stereo spin number two, when Mom said, "This sounds a lot like a lot of stuff I like, is it an old album?" and I said "No, it's from the future" and she said "Oh, the website—but why would you like this? It's not rap" and I said "The guy has set himself up to be the type of songwriter that probably sings about nothing at all, but people still obsess about the 'profound'" (fingers making rabbit ear shapes) "meaning of his stuff, and the interconnections between his songs, and albums, and stories, and plus it reminds me of when I was 8 and you and Dad would play records in our basement" and she said "Yeah, me too, except a lot of those records weren't quite as …, …, … poetic, I guess" and I almost said "I dunno, I mean, 'Hot Legs' lasted, right?" but didn't. When that conversation happened, during "3000 Flowers," around the time when Dad commented "The singer guy just said 'Hey that's good' to his band during a really nice part of the song, like Ray Charles did sometimes, except he had everyone in the studio with him all at once" and all I could think about was how that little "live" moment got recorded into a "studio album," and will stand out as a "unique" moment in the record for that one reason, and maybe might be the most personal thing that Bejar has ever recorded, but maybe not, we'd have to show him inkblots in order to find out, I got really confused about how nostalgia can smooth over sensitive spots (even making curse words ok for a bit). And how both remembering and forgetting old music can make new music better, and how having your hand held throughout an entire album is equal parts pushing and pulling, and how all of that bleeds together, risking to make no sense, unless you do actually push for your share of the record, and how that can be an excuse, or a challenge, depending on the audience.

CHAD VANGAALEN:
SKELLICONNECTION

Scott Reid & Aaron Newell
10 March 2006

This could've been so much more complicated. After introducing himself with 2004's endlessly charming *Infiniheart*, Chad Van-Gaalen originally planned to flip his ambitious indie folk-rock persona altogether with a sophomore effort described as "nothing but experimental piano compositions with drum machine accompaniment." No vocals, no melody, and, judging by how high up the Zappa scale leftover segues "Systemic Heart" and "Dandrufff" register, not much structure, either.

He eventually scrapped the idea, probably realizing the only way he could sell fewer records would be to follow-up his debut with experimental drum-'n-piano, a move that would also test the patience of his current small legion of fans, still processing his last record. So, once again embracing his more palatable side, he turned to plan B: mining the same hundreds-plus backstock of songs from which he'd tediously pieced together *Infiniheart* (says Chad: "it was like pulling hundreds of teeth"), while also mixing in a handful of new recordings made since that album's initial release. Even with the inclusion of some new material, it's probably best to think of *Skelliconnection* (2006) as being to *Infiniheart* what *Amnesiac* (2001) was to *Kid A* (2000): not so much a progression as an extrapolation, an offering from an artist who, by the very nature of his one-guy-in-a-bedroom aesthetic, should be telling us so much about himself when, really, his material has yet to enter real time. If Infiniheart made you wonder what was at the bottom of VanGaalen's murky pool of material, *Skelliconnection* deepens the well, stirs the waters, and offers a snorkel-shaped question mark: "Who the fuck is this guy?"

You can take some cues from the bio: Chad comes from Calgary, Alberta, a conflicted, mid-size city that's now spoonfed Canadian oil money, and is situated around a beautiful river, inside one of Canada's most breathtaking mountain panoramas. So we have a tall, lanky Albertan who can wake up to a postcard every day, who sees an influx of technology and machinery and modern excess in this environment, and who seems to want to take as much inspiration as possible from his surroundings. He spends his fantastical days drawing and animating and making music, lots and lots of music, collected like diary entries and handed out, up until now, on homemade CD-Rs wrapped in pages from old National Geographic magazines. Focus in closer on his art, and his personalities spiral out like, to use his own simile against him, "Those new floating highways." As an artist and animator his work ranges from fascinatingly creepy animated videos featuring combinations of birds and entrails and engines and pistons and flowers and human faces, to album covers/liner artwork mixing childlike scribbles with colourful, intricately detailed paintings. As a musician, he's pretty much whatever he wants to be: the reserved folkie, the exaggerated riff-rocker, the indie-pop eccentric, *The Eraser* (2006). Hell, on one as-of-yet unreleased track, he even takes on freestyle rap (sample: "You don't want to mess with my insane unruliness"; he also rhymes "griddle" with "fiddle"). Seriously.

It's this kind of intrinsic disregard for musical template that keeps VanGaalen from falling into cliche categorical foxholes, writing samey songs in the same samey styles. Of course, it doesn't hurt that his tunes are all beautifully sung (often layered, a wavering falsetto over his mild tenor) and cleverly arranged, as only he could, since he builds most of his instruments. And though he has access to and can play more instruments than he's able to list in the liner notes (maybe he should consider one of those Architecture in Helsinki dot-charts, except he's just one person, not eleven), he rarely uses the same combination or effect twice. Instead, he's constantly changing setups and approaches to his recording, toying with each song's atmosphere and tone to keep it all from getting monotonous, especially when he's retreading similar ground. Just compare the light, sole bass drum and electric-guitar-as-muted-trumpet bounce of "Graveyard" with "Wing Finger's" loose, rhythmic banjo and "Rolling Thunder's" haunting, nearly claustrophobic vocal mix. He's not always so subtle in how he presents his songs—e.g. the pounding distortion of "Flower Gardens" or nuzzling synths of "Red Hot Drops," the kind of stuff that pops out even on cursory listens—but, like *Infiniheart*, a great deal of this record's appeal rests in its smallest details and touches, which can be as affecting as moments like "Dead End's" operatic chorus, just way easier to miss.

Which may explain why VanGaalen, always standing on the other side of your kaleidoscope, can't seem to sell a damn record, and is once again subject to a confoundingly-discrepant slate of critical response. Sad but true: despite VanGaalen's admirable tour schedule and the just-enough passionate press presenting him as a new "Outsider Icon," his profoundly-rewarding *Infiniheart* has sold a paltry 2600 copies since its re-release exactly one year ago. Granted, that could be par for the re-released indie-weirdo debut album course, but that figure still feels low—insulting, even—especially if you've already been circulated through *Infiniheart* and have yet to shake the chill. The positive side is that it's a sure bet that those 2600 people have been wholly-swept-away in that record, and can therefore relate VanGaalen's plight to the few other slow-to-go "artistic" musicians whose brilliance is acknowledged over a timeline of water-torture drops, rather than a slippery-slope-making mudslide. Not to put too much emphasis on "getting it," but, in this case, to know is usually to love. Or fall victim to, since VanGaalen's Buckley-like banshee chinook, wielding semi-conscious dreamspeak, claws, climbs, and burrows into your brain where it hibernates and sheds new-Canadian-gothica in its sleep.

Skelliconnection largely recaptures what made that debut so easy to obsess over. It expands on the same playfully dour Canadian Gothorama ground enough to make it clear why he wanted to get more of this work off of his chest, and out into peoples' heads, before pushing forward with new material. It just doesn't get us much closer to knowing where, exactly, all this is going. At this point, from this artist, comfortable in the catalogued-cocoon that he's built on his own terms, anything seems possible. Beyond what he's already accomplished with just two records, knowing that his next release is as likely to channel Glenn Branca as it is Hayden is a big part of what makes VanGaalen such a unique, compelling talent— one certainly worth some tangible fan support this time around, if not just so he doesn't get dropped by his (kind, hopefully understanding) label. The last thing anyone wants is to be in a 2600-person line-up for one of 50 CD-Rs of his next release. And since it is indeed true that his music could be even more than it already is (which, again: beautiful, meticulous, a little creepy), there's no need to let such potential languish, ignored for lack of, well, heart.

TIMELINE OF A CMG REVIEW

Christopher Alexander
2005

MONDAY
5:00 PM PDT – Deadline for review
5:15 – Download album slated to review
5:40 – Listen to first track; wrinkle nose; search allmusic.com for a pic.
6:00 - 11:59 – *The West Wing* Marathon on Bravo

TUESDAY
12:00AM - 1:00AM – The rest of *West Wing* Marathon
1:05 – Listen to Warren Zevon
2:00 – 3:00 Cruise MySpace.com.
4:00 – Sleep
1:00 PM – Wake up
1:05 – Check e-mail; nothing from Scott or Aaron, phew!
1:06 - 4:00 – Cruise MySpace.com
4:15 – go to Cokemachineglow e-z board
4:16 - 5:00 – download music other people are slated to review
5:01 – Meet friends at Taco Del Mar
7:00 – Come home, *West Wing* on Bravo
8:12 – e-mail from Scott, subject reads "anything for this week?" do not open
8:13 – resume search of allmusic.com
8:15 – search metacritic.com
8:40 – compile best excerpts from every review

8:45 – Google search

9:15 – feel antsy, want to listen to music. Listen to *Beggars' Banquet* (1968)

10:00 – find band/artist's bio on label web-site; copy desired quotable passage and paste onto word file containing highlighted sections from other reviews

10:15 – begin to reword other passages

11:00 – feel pretty good about review's progress; e-mail Scott and Aaron swearing that the article is already done, cite arcane problems with router, give arbitrary day and time they'll see the review

11:01 - 11:59 – Watch downloaded *West Wing* episodes on computer.

WEDNESDAY

12:00 AM - 5AM – Watch downloaded West Wing episodes on computer.

5:15 – Sleep

3:30 PM – Wake up

4:00 – Head out for job hunt

4:15 – Return from job hunt claiming it's too late to look for work anyway; complain to girlfriend about latest atrocities from the Bush administration

5:01 – Call Taco Del Mar; ask if they deliver

5:02 – Dejected; walk into kitchen and prepare third bowl of ramen

5:23 - 7:00 – Cruise MySpace.com

7:01 – *West Wing* on Bravo

8:00 – Another e-mail from Scott, and this time Aaron. Don't open.

8:02 – Update Livejournal; complain of ennui and stress

8:15 – Reopen Word document containing everyone else's review; rewrite to your satisfaction.

9:00 – The review now half-done; listen to album all the way through

9:45 – Great, another band that sounds like Olivia Tremor Control/

Gang of Four/Modest Mouse/Pavement/The Cure.

9:46 – Relisten to album; find song with obvious chord changes, make a note to grandstand your "musical background"

9:57 – Gaze lovingly at own photo next to music degree; admire the imperceptible way elbow obscures the word "Community" from the diploma

10:30 – Ramen bowls 4-7

11:00 - 11:59 – Cruise MySpace.com

THURSDAY

12:00 AM - 2:30AM – MySpace.com

2:31 – Implore girlfriend to write review under own byline

2:38 – Assure girlfriend it was a joke, beg her to stop throwing own clothes out window

3:00 – Write Aaron (but not Scott) saying it's on its way.

3:15 – Go to bed.

1:00 PM – Wake up.

1:30 – Check mail; nothing from CMG people; mail from mom asking how fictitious job interview went; fail to remember intricate web of deceit woven over last two years

1:35 – Consult notes, journals, and helpfully detailed map of said deceit; interview was for another coffee house; use details from real interviews along with fiction; wonder if mom knows all this and is merely watching me dig myself deeper

1:40 – Return to review

1:41 – Consult Nick Kent's *The Dark Stuff* (1994) for sentences to steal

2:30 – Consult thesaurus

3:00 – Contrive a way to insert "vesuvian" into review of pop record

3:30 – Insert it anyway

4:00 – All done but the ending

4:01 - 6:30 – Cruise Myspace.com

6:31 – Letter from Scott; this usually means site has been updated

6:32 – Site has been updated; notice unsightly "coming soon" graphic where your blurb should be

6:35 – Mom calls; relate prevaricated story; consider asking her if she's only watching me suffer; ask for money instead

7:00 - *West Wing* on Bravo

8:00 – Head out for food; decide Taco Del Mar is too far; head to closer and cheaper Taco Bell

9:00 – Return to computer, roll up sleeves to work on ending

9:15 – Halfway through ending, a spark in brain for a funny, much more accurate and original review

9:16 - 9:59 – Ignore spark

10:00 – Spark has become a piercing wail; grab hair and scream that you want it over

10:05 – Read work so far to girlfriend; float other idea by her as well

10:10 – Girlfriend says new idea far better to the derivative work already completed

10:11 – Break up with girlfriend

10:12 – Beg for reconciliation; hands off genital region

11:00 – Heal; rewrite review from scratch

FRIDAY

4:00 AM – Finish work at 7:00 AM Scott's time, where he's been working for an hour and waiting. Send draft deeply unsatisfied with finished result and laughably contrived play/article/debate format

4:15 – Go to bed; await firing

11:00 – Wake up

11:13 – find a number of positive e-mails in my inbox

11:18 – check e-z board; staff loves it too

12:00 PM – come out of shock

12:01 - 11:59 – forget next deadline is only two days away; cruise myspace.com

AMERICAN GRAY SPACE

Andre Perry
2 November 2007

"Nigger music," he said.

He paused and thought deeply for a moment. "Yeah, that's what we do: full on nigger music. It's fucking great."

I wasn't quite sure what to say so I leaned into the couch and mumbled something like, "That sounds fascinating. I've got to come see that sometime."

San Francisco hipsters filled the corners of the dark apartment. Outside, a light rain came down around the city. Conversations oscillated between fashion and music. I could have talked to so many people but I had chosen this skinny musician who had tried to French kiss me earlier. In that moment, hHe seemed like a true artist to me – someone who created, revised, destroyed, and rebuilt in an effort to understand the world. And, he played nigger music. Was it a travesty or a triumph that this skinny, five o'clock shadowed white guy had so comfortably described his band's style of music to me, a skinny, five o'clock shadowed black guy, as none other than "nigger music"? He apparently didn't know what else to call it. He said that his rock band, Mutilated Mannequins, constructed lyrical diatribes on racism, pairing them with gripping art-rock freak-outs. He was so sincere, calm, and honest. His eyes honed in on me, his confidence unwavering. His philosophies unfolded before me: "We are doing important shit, man. Rethinking the whole world. The whole fucking paradigm."

He went on describing his music. After sometime his words echoed listlessly like the distant pitter-patter of rain on the windowsill. I thought about punching him in the neck. I was in a state of existential shock. Lifting up from my body I considered that I needed to spend less nights like this: 26 years old, going to work, making music, barely sleeping, and then going out just to hear someone talk about nigger music. The age-old question lingered: would it ever be possible for a non-black person to throw around the word "nigger" in a non-malicious sense? Does the weight of such a word truly vary with context or is it a shotgun shell whenever it gets fired into the air? And, damn, sometimes it takes a minute to figure out how they're shooting. Former NAACP representative, Julian Bond said that the 2nd Civil Rights Movement will be harder because the "Whites Only" signs have been taken down. Yet their shadows remain firmly placed to doorways and water fountains. How do you challenge a ghost when you can't even touch it?

I visited the University of Virginia when I was 19. I was a freshman studying at Princeton but I joined some friends for a road trip. The campus stood as a memorial to Thomas Jefferson – political leader, slave owner, and sexual violator. I stumbled down fraternity row, drunk and foggy, beneath a warm blanket of Gentlemen Jack Daniels. I had chased down the whiskey with half a case of Natural Light. Then I had lost my friends at the Delta Kappa Epsilon fraternity house. That was the place where they tossed couches from the second-floor balcony when they get bored.

I had spent the day tracking down friends from D.C. In high school, our class was so small that there wasn't much room for segregation. White kids and kids of color spent a lot of time together – we were mostly all friends. Yet, just several months removed from that privileged prep school experience I found that all of my friends had splintered into different circles in Charlottesville. If they did not see each other because of their different academic and social interests, I could understand that, but the realization that white and black people did not congregate socially at such a distinguished school shocked me. I had been fast asleep and suddenly I was awake. As I grew older and more explicitly understood the context in which the University of Virginia had been conceived, it was my early-college naivete that would prove more shocking. It is a school and community that pays homage to a remarkable, elite, and intelligent hero, Thomas Jefferson, who, in the midst of his accomplishments, embraced the ownership (and sexual predation) of slaves towards his own benefit. The system, from its inception, was complex and cracked.

As the evening descended, I conspired to find my college friends who I had parted from earlier. In an age before cell phones, I asked a group of white-shirt, dark-tie frat boys sitting on the steps of another fraternity if they had seen about four or five guys in Princeton t-shirts walking by.

One of them stepped forward, stars and bars glistening behind his eyes, and pointed in a direction that I had no intention of following. He said, "A bunch of black guys came by here ten minutes ago. They went that way."

He might have been helpful had I specifically inquired about black friends, but I hadn't and his assumptions bred something foul in my stomach. He had used the golden sword of 21st century racists. He had called me a nigger without even using the word. The invisible noun: it just needs to be insinuated—a subtle threat of a bomb that could go off at any moment. I waved my hand at him, pushing away his advice, a dismissal of what he had to offer. I could have taken them on. I could have traded in bloody teeth for intangible pride. I could have found out if they have "Whites Only" signs in Valhalla.

2.

Wait, do you remember the first time you put that record on? Maybe it was a CD or a tape. My roommate had picked up the LP from a San Francisco street vendor for 99 cents: Elvis Costello's *This Year's Model* (1978). That picture on the front is priceless: Elvis bent over a camera taking a picture of you, turning the listener into his model. The album's third track, "The Beat," captures the essence of new wave music as well as Blondie, the Cars, and Talking Heads had done in entire albums. I used to spin "The Beat" and other songs off *This Year's Model* at late-night house parties just when the makeshift dance-floor of someone's apartment needed one more momentous lift. That song, no, that whole album, was always reliable. I even owned the CD, the expanded edition with all of the demos and b-sides.

One day a friend told me the old story about Elvis Costello calling Ray Charles a "blind, ignorant nigger" during a drunken argument with Bonnie Bramlett and Stephen Stills in a Columbus, Ohio bar in 1979. When I heard the story, my blood froze up like Arctic pistons. I stopped listening to Costello immediately. Listening to his music would have felt like a betrayal to my identity, my people. I leafed through numerous articles on the Internet detailing Costello's frequent attempts to reckon with and apologize for the incident. Costello, whose actions have often put him on the side of peace, social justice, and equality, has witnessed the weight of his words follow him into his golden years – as recently as 2015 he discussed and apologized for his drunken, youthful missteps in an interview with ?uestlove. Even though I wouldn't listen to him, I couldn't bring myself to throw out his albums. I was caught somewhere between my love for the music and a mistake that I couldn't forgive. *This Year's Model* remains tucked away in my long shelf of vinyl.

Mick Jagger famously referred to black women as brown sugar in a song of the same name, then managed to squeeze out a phrase about "ten little niggers sittin' on da wall" in "Sweet Black Angel" (confusingly in a song about Civil Rights activist Angela Davis) and came full-circle with the revelation that black girls wanna get fucked all night long on 1978's "Some Girls" (a song that disparaged women of all backgrounds).

Nevertheless, there was a period when I listened to the Stones all of the time and something about it killed me. Why should Costello get the sanction while the Stones have access to my stereo? Maybe their oft-professed debt to black musicians excuses their racial errs. (Wait, Costello loves black American music.) Perhaps it's the fact that they have been roundly sexist, racist, and offensive to practically everyone on Earth. (But Costello appears to be one of the nicest people in the music industry.) It certainly must be their combination of irresistible hooks, intriguing decadence, and unapologetic rock n' roll clichés that make them the bad guys that I hate to love. (Isn't "Allison" one of the catchiest pieces of pop ever written?)

Rap artists Mobb Deep's second album, *The Infamous* (1995), is one of the best albums of the last century. It offers a gritty portrayal of New York life, possessing a distinct literary honesty akin to Lou Reed's impressions of the city through his solo work and albums with The Velvet Underground. If I dared to count the number of times they throw out the n-word on that album, I would find myself quite busy, perhaps needing a secretary. But why would I count? Their n-bombs and tales of urban violence don't bother me when I'm listening to the music. Even though they had art-school backgrounds, their drug-lord sound is so convincing that it doesn't matter. When I think about Mobb Deep and their Infamous album (and really, any number of rap albums can serve as the control here), my reasonable side tells me that I should be bothered by their loose use of "nigger" – trap talk and misogyny aside. But it sounds so good. I catch myself in the car or listening to my music on my phone rattling off lines like, "This nigga that I'm beginning to dislike, he got me fed/If he doesn't discontinue his bullshit, he might be dead," as if they were my own.

Rap producer Dr. Dre makes records that millions of people can dance and bob their heads to. He's been doing it for years through the voices of a variety of rappers: Ice Cube, Snoop Dogg, Eminem, Kendrick Lamar. He is a legend. Yet he was also a member of a band called N.W.A (Niggaz wit Attitudes) and produced an album called *Niggaz4Life* (1991). Does he feel at this point in his career, when he can roll up to the Grammy Awards looking dapper and decidedly un-gangsta, that he is a nigger for life? This is the man who co-founded Beats Audio, a company purchased by Apple for several billion dollars. Or does no amount of corporate wealth and industry success protect a luminary even like Dr. Dre?

Perhaps in the entertainment world it doesn't matter what you call yourself as long as you manufacture hits for the executives. (Good reviews from the critics are a plus, but only optional.) And if to Dr. Dre and others, the "nigga4life" lifestyle means casual sex, getting high, and flaunting money, then perhaps it can be a black term for rock star; in which case, Keith Richards, Tommy Lee, and Dave

Navarro all could have had guest spots on the *Niggaz4Life* album.

How does the rest of the country consider Dr. Dre? How might a white, rap-listening college graduate working on Capitol Hill feel about a rap icon? Does this white college grad consider the image of the African-American portrayed in hip-hop when considering larger racial issues? Or does he even care to mix his art with politics and ethics? Maybe after all it's just music and the ethos of rock and roll filtered through the African-American experience comes out in such a way that niggers are homies are bros are pals are dudes are your crew. What are the nationwide effects if everyone, not just black people, buys into this logic? Or is it already selling? Rap music rarely goes multi-platinum without white money. So where are the white listeners – the ones who roll down the street en route to middle class jobs in their trucks shaking the whole block with the bass and rhymes of A$AP Rocky, Rick Ross, and the Game – where are they when it is time to stand in the streets for justice, for the requiems of Sandra Bland, Michael Brown, and the ever-expanding roll call of innocent lives consumed by hate? Where are they when they just need to vote for the right person? To have it both ways, for all of us, is a distinct privilege that we should never invoke.

3.

My brother, a successful lawyer, was sitting in a Dunkin' Donuts in a suburb of Boston, with his two and a half year-old daughter. He assumed a high school football game was going on nearby when a group of teenage African-American males walked into the shop and raised a little bit of juvenile hell. No, not guns and threats, just loud voices and lewd conversation: universal adolescent behavior. An older white man asked them to keep it down and one of them rallied back, "What's the matter, don't you have a real Dunkin' Donuts in your neighborhood?" As my brother began to pack up his things the boys left the shop. The manager, who my brother assumed to be Indian or Pakistani, promptly called the police.

My brother left before the police came but he relayed two thoughts to me over the phone. The first: why did those kids have to be so inappropriately unruly – don't they know the camera is always unfairly turned on them as young black bodies? The second: why the hell did the manager call the police? What were the police going to do? Nothing had really happened. No guns were pulled and no one was assaulted – though in this current era, such an encounter could have resulted in death. My brother felt burned by the kids for shaking the fragile image of black Americans and offended by the over-reaction from the store manager. He hadn't done anything. He had just shown up for donuts and coffee. And that old white man, what exactly did he think? Did he see two different types of people in his mind or were the rowdy kids and my brother cut from the same rock?

From Kaplan's popular study guide, <u>The Real GRE: Surviving the American Social Landscape</u>

The New New Analogy

Directions: Pick the best answer and then write an explanation for the answer you choose. If you are having difficulty forming your thoughts then read the sample answers provided below.

NIGGER : BLACK PERSON ::

A. TYPE A : TYPE B

B. PAST : FUTURE

C. INFERIOR : SUPERIOR

D. PART : WHOLE

E. ALL ANSWERS ARE CORRECT

Sample Answers:

TYPE A : TYPE B

Rapper Lil Jon grew up in a stable, middle class environment. Will Smith did as well. Both entertainers are smart and successful and their professional end-goals run parallel: amassing significant amounts of wealth; but Will Smith has moved down a path that has allowed him to sustain a black identity without being stereotyped as ghetto or gangster. He moves seamlessly between different performances, from pairing with Martin Lawrence in the action-comedy *Bad Boys* (1995) to working with Donald Sutherland in the art-house theatrics of *Six Degrees of Separation* (1993) to big-screen, science-fiction blockbusters like *Men in Black* (1997). White people love Will Smith. They buy tickets to his movies. In contrast, Lil Jon has cashed in on a more street-level aesthetic, less concerned with established "etiquette" or playing it both ways. In the early 2000s, Lil Jon called his southern blend of hip-hop "crunk." With genre classics like, "Real Nigga Roll Call" and "Move Bitch" it sold a lot of units. Without seeing the market reports, it is safe to assume that black rap fans weren't the only ones picking up these records. Again, it takes white American dollars for records to go platinum. White people loved Lil Jon. They bought copies of his records. They consumed his reflection of life as never-ending gangsta-party.

PAST : FUTURE

Q-Tip, the talented rapper from A Tribe Called Quest, considered the n-word's history and the politics of its use within black culture in "Sucka Nigga" – the meditation so important that he raps the same verse twice. The song ends with a vocal sample the denoting, "You're not any less of a man if you don't pull the trigger [referring to the use of the n-word]/You're not necessarily a man if you do." In his own practice as a rapper, Q-Tip has both used the word, over the years, in a number of different ways, sometimes critiquing aspects of African-American culture and at other times as a term of endearment. In "Sucka Nigga" he raps, "Yo I start to flinch as I try not to say it/But my lips is like the oowop as I start to spray it." Both the embrace and the regret are palpable as Q-Tip attempts to walk the tight-rope of this heavy cultural question. By putting off his termination of the word in his lyrics, is Q-Tip (and other rappers) acting a bit like our founding fathers: at the birth of our nation they decided to hold off on solving the problem of slavery, even though they knew it was an issue that would eventually have to be dealt with. Who forms a republic based on equality and freedom and also has slaves?

INFERIOR : SUPERIOR

Chris Rock, in his stand-up comedy film, *Bring the Pain* (1996), remarked about a civil war occurring within the black community. He said there was a war between black folks and niggers. Via the hard binary of his perspective: black folks represented reasonable American citizens while niggers reflected an approach of playing outside of the rules of day-to-day life in American society. It still stands as one of the most public and accessible essays on oft-discussed rifts within the black American community. By using the terms "blacks" and "niggers" he immediately identified a class issue within the community — the difference in class being: are you capable of acting in a way that is deemed acceptable by Western societal standards (i.e., the identity crushing step towards assimilation) or will you choose an alternate path (and forever be kept on the perimeter)? (Are these the only two choices?)

PART : WHOLE

As much as Chris Rock suggests that niggers are inferior to black people, by using the Civil War analogy he is also suggesting that they are part of a greater whole. And whether it was intentional or not, Rock's "joke" about the class structure of the black community applies to all Americans: class is an all-American issue. Each ethnic, religious, and social group is made up of a number of different parts that comprise the whole. After all, what would upstanding white people be without their white trash? They would all just be white – and it would be impossible for white people to define success within their own ranks if someone wasn't stereotypically getting drunk and knocking up their cousin in the trailer park. How socially successful can a professional black man or woman be if some other black person isn't around to tip the tables of ignorance? Human class structure requires us to draw these lines – and so often one's class is determined by their birth right. So how can black Americans fight the powers that be and still be human?

He played guitar and the name of his band was Mutilated Mannequins. They played nigger music. I am black and always looking for answers. I had no choice but to track them down.

On a foggy Saturday night I squeezed my way through the crowded bar of Edinburgh Castle in San Francisco's Tender-Nob district. Hipsters swelled around the bar, ordering up New Castle, High Life, and Guinness, throwing back Irish car bombs and cleaning up shots of whiskey. I came in uniform – the slightly torn blue jeans, the frayed prep-school sweater, and a scarf that identified me as a thinking man's hipster rather than a downtown, flophouse art-school casualty. Beer in hand, I stormed upstairs, alone and on a mission to see the Mannequins play their music, to convince me of their perverse Afro-centric cause.

The band's three members looked so intentionally special with their '80's lipstick and clothes tighter than the bodies they struggled and sometimes failed to cover. On first listen, the music didn't seem so much like black music or music at all. Rather it came off like a grating performance-art headache. Melodies were scarce and lyrics were rendered indecipherable underneath the screams and bellows of the singer's anguish. My "friend," who played guitar and tried to kiss me at late-night parties while telling me that his band played "nigger music," loomed in a corner of the stage bursting into epileptic theatrics from time to time. The keyboardist humped a synthesizer with his fists and occasionally pushed buttons on a drum machine.

Despite the noisy fuss, the singer was visually captivating: he was black with dreadlocks, all done-up with beautiful glam make-up, positively gay, loud, and possessed.

He sang: "Caucasian neocolonist/Wanting to freak with the freakest/Seeking and searching for the scariest/Thugged out nigga pussy terrorist. and he shouted: Welcome to the plantation/We the niggas sexing the nation/White folk, white folk be giving ovation like head/I guess we quite the sensation."

I talked to him for a bit after the show but in person he was much too art-scenester and I was too much of an indie-prepster; even our shared blackness and interest in music wasn't enough to make us want to hang out for more than five minutes. Yet from that night on, every time I saw him tucked into the corners of a San Francisco bar with a lover in his arm, we always nodded to each other—that ever-bonding "black man nod" to acknowledge: yes, I see you brother, and even though I'm wearing a skinny tie and listening to New Order and you're walking off with your analyst colleagues to a power lunch, I still got your back because, shit, we're black, and this shit is real from back-alleys to boardrooms.

I was intrigued by the motions of the Mutilated Mannequins' singer if not by his band's sounds. They pushed some cultural buttons from behind their wall of noise. Their lyrics attacked American racial issues head-on. Yet, I left the show feeling a little bit unsatisfied. They buried their diatribe under the noise. A passive listener could have missed it. I wondered and couldn't quite determine why the singer had given license to his arty white friends to play and promote his nigger music. I didn't want to listen to his friends as much as I wanted to read what he had to say. Perhaps he was afraid to state his case in such plain terms or maybe he was trying to represent the true nature of the race issue in America: a wealth of ideas covered up by white noise — screaming to be heard. And if it was nigger music then it was also American music. I would need to tell that to my late-night French-kissing friend when I saw him again.

I left the clamor of the Edinburgh Castle, walking back onto the streets of the Tenderloin where drinking, poverty, and drugs all converged. I moved into the night, continuing to run my fingers across the gray-skinned canvas on which many of our country's stories are painted.

THIS SCENE IS KILLING ME: AN EVENING WITH ROCK KILLS KID AND OTHER FINE INDIVIDUALS SUCH AS MYSELF

Andre Perry
21 December 2007

"It's Saturday night and indie rock is dying. Or maybe it's Tuesday or Thursday. I dunno. What's certain is that that this particular brand's been stiffening up for a couple of years now, its body destroyed by tired chord progressions, bands enforcing style over substance, and one too many nods to the New Wave, garage rock, or other "classic" genres. Of course, "classic" is a term and terms are what keep us sane, encapsulating zeitgeists into digestible touch-stones so the incomprehensible distance between what's available to listen to and what we actually are able to listen to isn't so daunting. Terms allow us History:

Long ago, there were visionaries: Velvets, Dylans, Dolls, and Pistols expanding the parameters of rock's sound by shrinking its restraint. Then there were true independents: Fugazis, Replacements, and Minutemen toiling their way across the country erecting a network for the underground. At some point, we took the word "indie" and applied it to the bands—Pavements, Dinosaurs, and Mice—that sounded different and embraced the ideals and techniques of our brick-laying heroes. Those bands further defined and enriched the underground network and re-imagined rock's possibilities. Simple enough.

This History, all of it, is a good thing. But somewhere along the road, the cool kids and the scene-makers, the suits and the promoters, caught on and not only made indie rock their soundtrack but embraced its style. It's difficult to pinpoint exactly when or where it started, maybe in Brooklyn and the Lower East Side, as hordes of middle-class post-college youth set up shop, avoiding Generation X. The intentions at first must have been genuine—we like this music, let's celebrate it—but then independence caught on and that's when the people who make money had enough sense to sign the Strokes.

Yes, the very word "independent" is at stake, ready and willing to be commodified into a term that simply signifies the young apart from the old; true independent and original music continues on, perhaps more than ever in basements and concert halls across the country. But this thing called "indie rock" is more than just a useful catchall phrase to describe new music. Like hip-hop, it has become marketable pop culture, a mainstream-leaning product. You don't need Sub Pop to put out an indie band. Warner Bros. and his colleagues do it just as well. In 2007 they know what it looks like and what it sounds like and who to sell it to. We even sell it ourselves. Vice magazine shits on indie culture and then, as only pure irony would have it, picks it up, eats it, and puts it in your local boutique, at which point you pick it up and laugh at a picture of your coke-addled counterpart in some or another American city.

It's easy to unfold layers of vitriol upon such useless outfits as the Bravery and Moving Units, exposing them as the problems with indie rock. But there's always been bad music, so we can't point fingers at the Bravery for making indie a dirty word. We can blame the scene that surrounds and supports this bad music: clubs and parties packed with hype-fueled expectations and the fans with thick white or black wristbands, retro clothes, angular haircuts, make-up to cast them as vampires, and enough coke to put a Bret Easton Ellis protagonist on edge. I cough bird flu on them, those wayward acolytes so eager to rally around whatever bullshit the bodega sells them. Is it just plain over? Should we all move on? Yet another critical cliché, suggesting that everything is so do-or-die. Indie Rock Is Dead! Long Live Indie Rock! What am I, an Arcade Fire record?

Some time ago, whatever night that was, I was pushing around the streets of San Francisco minding my business. Thousands of rock fans had just finished a day of partying at alternative radio station Live 105's annual BFD rock festival featuring the Strokes, Yeah Yeah Yeahs, Echo & The Bunnymen, and more. You wouldn't have caught me dead at that concert. It was at Shoreline, an unpleasantly large venue outside of the city that dumps most of its ticket holders onto a vast lawn. What a waste: all of those bands, some good, others washed-up, and you can't even see them from where you're standing. ok, maybe if you had given me a free ticket I would have gone. But you definitely wouldn't have caught me at the BFD after-party taking place at the ultra-hip downtown club Mezzanine and featuring here-today/gone-tomorrow buzz band of the month, Rock Kills Kid. Well okay, I was at the after-party, but that didn't mean I liked it.

I'm not a scenester, I promise. I don't have the fashion-sense; by the time I hear the new it's already old, and I can only stay up late once a week these days. That aside, on some masochistic level I can't stand to miss the party I hate, just to tell people I was there and hated it. Furthermore, just being at the hated party establishes that I knew about it and that I could get in and that I could rightfully hate it. Public appearance is essential and private dissatisfaction is a posture that many of us not-so-secretly relish. Scenesters only disappear from the scene to make a statement: they've gone into exile, they've died, they will return with a new look, a new sound, a new stack of rare mash-up piled into their iPods, and as expected the sheep will follow. It's all very morbid.

My buddy Kevin had convinced me to accompany him after someone put us on the list. We slid past the line and into the unremarkable cavern that is the Mezzanine. It's just one big clinical room. Everything is synthesized, from the "mysterious" red lighting to the mist that floats through the air. It felt like a movie set, the one they use when the romantic leads do some dirty dancing in a hip, techno nightclub. A hot girl with a punkish leather skirt and pink hair brushed by us and grimaced. I think it was her way of smiling.

We walked over to the smoking area, a well-lit, open-air zone that was caged off so no one could get into the club from the street. Seeing it packed with human beings sucking on nicotine brought on a flashback to a Harper's article I read about the pork industry: the modern pig lives in a cage not much bigger than the pig itself. It shits on the floor and moves about nervously trying to figure out what to do with its limited existence. That punk chick with pink hair looked much better in the dark.

Kevin pointed to a round, sweaty kid with a bowtie and slightly maniacal grin. He laughed, "Yeah he was at my apartment last weekend doing coke until sunrise with all of his friends. These fuck-ing hipsters always leave such a goddamn mess. You wake up with baggies and beer cans all over the place." Yes Kevin, but you invited them over and secretly I kind of wished I had been there.

Andre Perry 59

Out of duty we checked out the end of Rock Kills Kid's set. It was awful, as if the band had been pre-packaged for the soundtrack to *Laguna Beach* or its cheeky Los Angeles sequel *The Hills*. People were dancing and by all accounts loving it. You may wonder how Rock Kills Kid, let alone *Laguna Beach* or *The Hills*, even sneaks itself into an article about the state of indie rock? Did the infiltration begin with *The O.C.*'s appropriation of the Walkmen? (Or do we question the Walkmen's willingness to be appropriated by anything with a pulse?) Just think about the cool kids and remember that they are in power. Little babies with camo diapers and platinum Zippos, a funny image that allows Kevin and I to continue fantasizing:

Some young writer in L.A. says: this is what I like and since I am "the kids" this is also what the kids like. This young writer, this Young Turk hears "Fake Empire" and damn does it make sense to place it in the scene where the girls find that their boyfriends are cheating on them. Then there's a Hollywood executive smiling as the Young Turk explains to him how the company will enact a hip and smart MySpace or blog campaign to convince the world to buy into this band that wrote this damn sensical song. The Turk tells the old man, who is incidentally eating a steak sandwich and smoking a cigar, that, "This is the 'indie' thing sir. This is what they want: tight jeans and coke."

"Well if that's what they want then sell it to them, Charlie," the executive replies. He turns to his window as the Young Turk leaves his office, looking out the window, taking in the ants below running through arteries of industry. He chuckles to himself, "Heh, when I was young they just called it rock."

Kevin and I had an idea: I produced a pen and a pad from my back pocket and we scribbled some fan mail for the band. It read:

Wow, you guys play so well! Too bad your music is the most derivative played-out shit we've heard in months. Cheers! :)

We left the note on top of the keyboard while the keyboardist was playing guitar. He smiled from a distance thinking, no doubt, that we'd left him our girlfriends' phone numbers. Looking for trouble elsewhere, we headed backstage. I lied to the bouncer, put on my mask, and told him I was a writer for Pitchfork there to interview Rock Kills Kid post-show. "Somehow, sir, I've misplaced my press pass." He stared at us, poker-faced and said, "I'm sorry. No pass, no entry."

A woman walked up to us with faux-blond hair and a worn-in face. I placed her as older, shifting with the scene as new fashions turned over but keeping her social-climbing core intact. Her whole demeanor was napalm. "Who in the fuck are you guys? If you're not in the fucking band, then get the fuck out!"

Where did she get the nerve? From what I could tell she didn't even work at the venue. A friend of ours in one of the BFD festival bands eventually saw us and waved us in. The bouncer apologized and sent us upstairs to mingle with the elite. The VIP lounge was split into a few different spaces with one area overlooking the dance floor of the Mezzanine; VIPs with PBRs laughed at the LFBs (less fortunate below) like Roman royalty considering the plebes. Tucked behind the lounge was a packed hallway leading to green rooms for the bands.

I moseyed on into Rock Kills Kid's room and chomped down on

some carrots from their fancy veggie platter. I swiped a water bottle and surveyed my surroundings. Hipsters abounded: young female fashionistas with haircuts from a book of lost geometry shapes; boys in their skinny-rocker jeans, myself included; some wearing the aforementioned one-color leather wrist bands, myself not included. Conversational marionettes swinging back and forth on their strings. The same setlist a different night, a different club. While 75% of the people backstage don't know shit about anything, it's all about looking confident and acting like you know shit about something. Take the situation by the balls, son, and look like a rock star, or a label rep, or a promoter, or a groupie who knows about the after-after party and has connections to all of the drugs. If you can adopt the look of confidence, then others will assume you're running the show in some sort of capacity. I was just a guy eating carrots, wearing faded black jeans and a navy-blue hoodie. But damn did I look serious with those carrots.

Across the room I noticed the lead singer from Rock Kills Kid appearing adolescent and lost at sea. I gathered up my courage. It was time for me to tell this kid that his band, well, um, sucked. He would be better, my ears would be cleaner, yes the whole world would be at ease if he just moved on and tried something else. I was there to break it to him while he was young and had time to explore other things. I walked over to him, extended my hand, and unraveled a rainbow of lies.

"Hi, my name is Andre and I've been sent by *Pitchfork* to review your band's show and write an article about it."

"Oh wow, cool. My name's Jeff. What'd you think?"

"You guys are fucking great. You're so tight. Good job."

Indie Scenster Backstage Party: 1

Andre Perry: 0

My integrity was at an all-time low. I couldn't bring myself to speak to Jeff honestly about his music. Or maybe I couldn't resist indulging in my P-fork bunburying. Perhaps he even knew I was a fraud but in his own ego-driven mind wanted to believe he was indeed being interviewed by *Pitchfork*. And I wanted him to think I was cool, and though I'd never met him before this night, that I was his friend in the kingdom of the backstage. With his cute smile and boyish looks, he should have been working at Disneyland: he was cut right off the white American chopping block. Let's frame him and put him up on the wall, says the Hollywood executive. This is Private Ryan and he plays rock 'n' roll. I wanted to hug him and save him from the machine that was telling him these are the clothes you should wear, this is the sound you're going for, and this is what your soul should smell like. But anyway, here's the interview.

"So do you want to interview me for the article?"
"Um, yeah, let's do a quick one. So how long have you been playing music and where did you grow up?"
"Man, I'm an L.A. kid. I've been doing this for years since I was 15 or 16."
"What's the goal?"
"You know, to make it. To get it out there so people can hear the music."
"How do you feel about the record?"
"I feel it's great. I think people will really enjoy it. But you know how it is. you never know. Maybe we'll get lucky."

I never listened to their album but I must that admit at the time the PR machine for this band was in full effect. I'd seen stickers for them on building walls around San Francisco, ads for them in music mags, and holy shit they'd run some pretty dominant banner campaigns on music websites. So I did find it possible that many people would hear their music and that some of them would really like the band. But why would they like it? Is it bad taste—I mean do people really want another year full of angular riffs, New Order synths, dance rock drumming, and lyrics that claim to be passionate, honest, and meaningful?—or is it because "trusted" media sources like MySpace tell them that they should digest Rock Kills Kid with a smile? At least their singer was a nice guy.

"Do you like the L.A. music scene? Are there bands you are into?"
"Yes, I love music in L.A. It's great."
"What do you think of Earlimart?"
"Who?"
"Earlimart. They're great. Kinda like Grandaddy."
"Huh?"
"What about Silversun Pickups? They're awesome."
"Um, I've never heard of them."

I couldn't even hold back my smirk. How could he live in L.A. and not even be aware of those bands? You know: the real indie stuff. Why hadn't the Mezzanine booked Earlimart to come and play? As I thanked him for the interview, Kevin came over and introduced himself, telling Jeff what a great show he played. When he walked away Kevin looked at me and asked, "Why the fuck were you talking to that guy? His band sucks."

Off to the toilet I went, presumably hoping to wash my hands of their insincere blood. Waiting ten minutes for a VIP bathroom struck me as backwards. Finally two attractive girls and a shirtless guy barreled out of the door with cocaine giggles falling from their mouths, noses, and souls. The party girls didn't even look at me and I almost got trampled as I tried to squeeze in. Some guy had been waiting behind me in line so I invited him in to share the facilities. "You take the sink and I'll take the toilet." He locked the door behind him and I realized it was the keyboardist/guitarist from Rock Kills Kid. Perhaps the fan mail had been a poor decision. Mid-leak, because I'm into keeping it real and all, I gave him a shout-out, "Hey great show, man."

He was cutting up on the sink counter. "Thanks bro. You wanna do a bump?"

I emerged from the bathroom arm-in-arm and exceptionally chum-chum with the keyboardist of a band that I didn't particularly like. I bid him farewell and felt around for Kevin's whereabouts. He was chatting it up with various people involved in the local music scene. Conversations circled around my head while I ran through questions I should have asked the band or even just the keyboardist. What becomes of him, well-dressed and playing a part in a corporately shaped indie success, doing coke and drinking beer for a living? Where is he in ten years? Certainly not doing session work for Steely Dan. But maybe he's backing up a mid-30s Julian Casablancas on a solo record produced in L.A. Yes, the Casablancas/Rock Kills Kid L.A. lost weekend of 2016. Pussycats revisited. Will I be at the after-party for their record release show or will I have moved on with the rest of the scene to promote and dance around another potential icon? Perhaps I can pencil both dates into my calendar of the future.

This must all come off a little hypocritical. Throwing stones and I was still there at the Mezzanine—am I still there?—plunk right in the middle of it all with a fresh PBR in one hand and ironic one-liners in the other. It seems fitting to recall such experiences as another year comes to a close and the corpse of my reason-to-be sinks a bit deeper into the earth. A girl I had met a few weeks earlier came over to say hello. I blanked on her name but I remembered she was in a band with a hot look, lots of local hype, and maybe three or four half-baked songs. She told me they'd already booked shows at some of the city's best clubs. Like the Mountain Goats said, "Shooting the sequel before the treatment's even finished." The scene was the main character and Kevin and I were just the willing details of another episode. We'd be back next week and perhaps even the next, waiting for producers to tell us to go someplace new. I turned and said, "Let's get the hell out of here."

THE MOUNTAIN GOATS: THE SUNSET TREE

Christopher Alexander
21 October 2007

WHY I LIKE THE MOUNTAIN GOATS IN GENERAL, AND
THE SUNSET TREE (2005) ESPECIALLY

A play in one act by Christopher Alexander

The curtain rises. We see a living room that is covered, wall to
floor, in wood paneling. If we were to see the floor, we would see it
was covered in deep scuff marks and scratches. These are wounds
from skateboard wheels, and in fact if we turn our attention to the
doorway, we see no less than two skateboards lying on the floor.
Both of them lay broken in half, so that all four pieces lie with their
nose pointed upwards like cannons. You may fail to notice them
among the pile of detritus, mostly containing crushed cans of Pabst
beer augmented with the occasional Harvey Weinhard bottle. In the
background there is a green couch, stiff with old sweat and littered
with magazines and ancient record sleeves. They fail to obscure
the stuffing falling out of the cushions, which has spilled over and
competes for space with the beer on the floor. In the foreground we
see a long picnic table, something that would be hilariously out of
place elsewhere, but here blends in with the empty picture frames
and tacked-up typewritten poems (the poems, it is worth noting, are
covered in their authors' blood. For dramatic effect, you understand). The table itself is covered with more of what's on the floor,

though the pile of molding dishes and fly-covered fast-food bags suggest that the kitchen is annexing the living room.

CHRISTOPHER walks through the room. He is a slight and bookish young man, Caucasian and bespectacled, clad in flannel pajamas. He surveys the wreckage, and then walks to stage center. He turns to address us directly.

CHRISTOPHER: Here's the set up: this is my living room. Now here's the punch-line: the other day I was wondering why John Darnielle's songwriting strikes such a chord in me.

The curtain falls.

THE END

Actually, I recently caught myself thinking that about X's first three records. It isn't just that the songs are conspicuously lived in, or the way it points out things I'd no idea that I already knew—that shock of recognition which is the hallmark of all great songwriting. No, what really got to me was their emphasis on narrative. You may remember narrative as the idea that a story should have a beginning, middle, and an end, and a character (sometimes the narrator) goes through a fundamental change. Maybe Black Flag's "Nervous Breakdown" is a better song, but to me there's something much more visceral about Exene Cervenka setting her kitchen on fire to escape the landlord ("We're Desperate"), or John Doe sleeping with a beautiful woman when he's living with one ("White Girl"), then Keith Morris yelling, "I'm crazy! I'm crazy! I just want to diiiiieeeee!" in my fucking face for ten minutes. That could also just be me.

So why am I talking about X in a piece about The Mountain Goats? The groups couldn't be more dissimilar: the punk quartet wrote songs about youthful alienation, adultery, spiteful relationships, the psychic implications of nihilistic debauchery, all with a strong sense of regional setting—oh, good, I have your attention again.

There are key differences, of course. "Los Angeles" told a xenophobic runaway's story in two short verses. Darnielle used nearly all 45 minutes of *Tallahassee* (2002) to express similar themes of metropolitan futility. Not that he didn't use every inch of the bigger canvas he afforded himself. Darnielle's lyrical range could start with a hilarious simile like, "Our conversations are like minefields: no one can find a safe way out of one yet," and turn on a dime to acerbic candor on the incredible "No Children": "In my life, I hope I lie / And tell everyone you were a good wife / And I hope you die / I hope we both die." *Tallahassee* remains the most sanguinary and unflinching record of a dysfunctional relationship in recent memory. The only thing I can think to compare it to is Edward Albee's *Who's Afraid Of Virginia Woolf?* (1962). He could've retitled it Long Day's Journey Into A Nightcap and no one would have noticed.

Tallahassee is an admittedly problematic place to begin discussion. After all, it's only the ninth album (to say nothing of singles and EPs) in a 14-year career. I do it here because the album demarcates a clear transition between phases, not simply because of its production value. Rather, having left his Panasonic behind, Darnielle also abandoned his characters and unreliable narrators for comparably uncharted waters: straight autobiography. It would be wrong to say that his first full bodied attempt, *We Shall All Be Healed* (2004), stumbled. It just lacked *Tallahassee*'s cohesion and erudition, or, when it didn't, strong hooks.

We Shall All Be Healed did signal a newfound focus on varying the instrumentation, even if, from a strictly musicological perspective, much of it was indistinguishable from the rest of his work. That's the first thing that's striking about *The Sunset Tree*: the arrangements on this record are spectacular. Darnielle is backed only by strings, "Eleanor Rigby" style, on "Dilaudid;" "Lion's Teeth" uses the strings and an electric guitar to achieve an unholy tension; "Dinu Lipatti's Bones" uses piano to achieve a kind of tenderness barely hinted at in something like "Tallahassee"; an organ lends majesty to the unfortunately titled "Hast Thou Considered The Tetrapod?" and takes an already gut-wrenching lyric somewhere else entirely. I don't know if this is due to Peter Hughes or producer John Vanderslice, but in terms of sheer musical heft, this is easily the best record Darnielle has ever done (romanticists of lo-fi aestheticism, "the tape hiss is its own instrument" fetishists be damned).

Still, the Mountain Goats have always been (at least roughly) analogous to the Leonard Cohen model: with lyrics this good, the music has no choice but to stay out of the way. *We Shall All be Healed* suggested a lack of confidence in writing personal material, or at least uncertainty. It was very competent, and wasn't wanting for great lines, but if one asks does it pass muster—meaning, whether or not Darnielle made his own life as rich and interesting as his fabrications—then a frank answer would be "no." Well, forget all of that. Darnielle has given us a story that is impossibly painful, subject matter that is unreasonable to expect the most self-referential artists to dissect, and he's fucking nailed it.

The Sunset Tree recounts the author's child abuse at the "swollen and thick-veined hands" of his step-father. Like his past work, there is no real story arc, and it's to Darnielle's eternal credit that many of his narratives work with people stuck in a pivotal moment of transition (see the famous "Going To" series). Rather, there is a series of connected and anachronistic vignettes that still achieves a cadence, not dissimilar to a Tarantino film (or Bergman's *Scenes From a Marriage* (1973), if you'd rather). Note how the most wrenching songs are smack in the middle of the tracklist. Note also that it's cushioned by the most soothing: "You Or Your Memory" and "Pale Green Things." That's no accident.

"This Year" seems like just another great Mountain Goats singalong. The narrator is 17 years young and can taste the scotch on his tongue, he can hear the engine hum, ho hum. There's a Mack truck around the corner. This year is year 17, one year to eighteen, one to freedom. "I'm gonna make it through this year if it kills me." It almost does. The end of the night is bad enough—"the scene ends badly, as you might imagine" is all he says of it. The police get involved on "Lion's Teeth," wherein he attacks his father by "grabbing the lion's tooth" and "holding on for dear life." What that alludes to is unclear — my guess is attempted strangulation — but the devastation isn't. "I'm going to regret the day I was born … there's no good way to end this."

"Up The Wolves" is rife with teenage revenge plots people like to think started with Columbine: "I'm going to bribe the officials / I'm gonna kill all the judges / It's going to take you people years to figure out all the damage." At its heart, though, is a child abandoned: "Our mother has been absent ever since we founded Rome / But there's gonna be a party when the wolves come home." They all pale next to "Tetrapod," a vivid recounting of a beating where Darnielle is more concerned with his stereo than his health: "Because it's the one thing that I can't live without / And I think about that, and I sorta black out."

It's perhaps elementary to discuss Darnielle's lyrical gift. It may even be useless to offer a comparison to the increasingly risible emo genre, something no Mountain Goats record is ever going to overtake in popularity. Still, it bears repeating: the reason Darnielle is taken seriously and Carrabba isn't (or at least not by anyone who won't soon outgrow him) is the narrative. Places, events, names: these are the essential pieces of mental furniture, as Allen Ginsberg might say. The play I've written is (hopefully) good for a laugh, but it doesn't contain an ounce of the blood — the anger, resentment, self-loathing and fatalism — that Darnielle would wrest from it when he's at top form. *The Sunset Tree* is top form.

R. KELLY f/ T-PAIN & T.I.: "I'M A FLIRT"

Eric Sams
31 January 2008

T.I.: "Look. I'm a pretty famous guy. I'm not ridiculous-cloistered-Jacko-mega-famous, but people know who I am. My music's pretty critically well received and my club hits, while having middling shelf lives, shake asses. So while R. Kelly indulges in his trademark megalomania let me use this dime store beat to offer you some sage advice. Don't bring your lady friend over to me for an introduction because you'll be inviting a comparison that isn't likely to put you in a favorable light. And while it's conventionally considered uncouth to straight out hijack someone's date, I won't be overly scrupulous in my efforts to deter her affections. Even if she's not a rap fan, even if she confuses me with Fabolous, it's not likely to end well for you. It's a weakness of mine. You've been warned: I'm a flirt."

T-Pain: "I'm not the most attractive cat in the club. However, this unfortunate fact could not be less indicative of the amount of ass I'm apt to pull out of any given singles-oriented establishment. You see, I reek of money. I'm a bling rapper. Braggadocio is not only excused in my line of work, it's absolutely fucking paramount. So in a sense, domineering the space with my advanced financial assets is a line item in my job description. So while R. Kelly croons his rapacious nonsense let me issue a caveat. A not entirely-unintentional side effect of this habit is that all of the attention at the club is directed toward me from the time I arrive until the time I leave. This, pal, likely includes your lady friend there. Now there's not much that either of us can do about the fact that wealth and its attendant power are almost universally attractive. I guess you could not bring her around to places where you knew that I was going to be, although that admittedly sounds like a somewhat ridiculous preventative measure. I'm just saying that it wouldn't be the first time that I've magnetized someone else's date away from them by sheer forceful swagger, despite the fact that I'm a chubby, dreadlocked southern guy in an oversized T-shirt. In the words of Three 6 Mafia: 'I ain't Denzel, but I know I'm a star.' In the words of me: 'I'm a flirt.'"

R. Kelly: "I'm gonna take your girlfriend, dog. I don't care if it takes me all night. I'm going home with your girl one way or another. I will walk up to you unawares and interrupt you in mid-sentence to make inappropriate sexual overtures toward any woman with whom I see you talking. I will steal her if you so much as turn your head to cough. You better get a seat at the bar, homey, because if you leave her to go get some drinks she'll be stowed away in my champagne-colored stretch Hummer by the time you get back. You'll be standing there holding a Stella Artois and a mango martini with a puzzled face on. Need to go to the bathroom? Hold it. What's more, this is your fault, son. You shoulda never brought her to the club tonight. Matter of fact, you should know better than to take her anywhere because of the off chance that I'll be within a five-block radius. If I have to follow you even unto the front steps of your building in order to snake this chick away from you I'll do it. Look into the void of my diamond-studded sunglasses. You know this to be true. It took seven hours for the barber to braid my hair like this, and it was all done for the single purpose of philandering other people's loved ones. You've seen the videos on the internet. I beat them charges cold, kid. I'm bulletproof. I'm the king of R&B. I'm a flirt."

WEEZER: WEEZER

Clayton Purdom & Alan Baban
23 June 2008

Really, we should be thankful. At last, at least, Cuomo has given us a steady rubric against which we can judge all other music; here he has bravely plumbed the depths of taste, defiantly applying his outrageous talent toward the most insidious music ever created. This is Cuomo, glasses aflame, shredding through the symbolism and equations and notepad schemata of one decade's worth of math; this is Cuomo embracing who he is, what he's become and why, actually, that's important full stop to our combined interests. This is Cuomo telling you he has something to say; this is Cuomo, and he's telling you to open your mouth. This isn't a toss-off: this is Cuomo explicit. This is Cuomo exploding. This, finally, is Cuomo in a gay cowboy hat.

We would that it were merely vacuous. *Make Believe* (2005), at least, was vacuous! And accurate, too: consistent with Weezer's decline, dutiful to those consistencies. It showed a band, which, though floundering in a post-*Pinkerton*ian universe, had at least come to terms with that decline. We don't listen to *Make Believe* (because it's awful), but we appreciate its overriding success (that it's awful). More than anything, it hit at a perfect nought-to-nought correspondence, the benchmark, really, for subsumed anonymity. They'd sanctioned Hugh Hefner, hiccupped a song for Shrek, posed on the cover as career bachelors in black. Cuomo was then celibate. Starting with the *Green Album* (2001), he'd written himself into oblivion and *Make*

Believe sounded like his conclusive submission from inside that artistic black hole. Not even the sound of his dying gasp escaped, so anonymous was its blurting.

But the *Red Album* is not vacuous. Instead this awfulness has form, heft, detail. The production is clean, though textured. We really hear these lyrics; they are right there in the mix. And the whole time, too: that heinous cover art! On *Weezer* (2008) our faces are pressed up against this sweltering, angry behemoth and shook like a dog in its filth, our own filth. This is Cuomo's festering tumor of sound, meted out in square punches with a bunch of square heads. This, in other words, is what the critics asked for last time we called shop. Return to the whimsy, Rivers! *Alone* (2007), which isn't even a real album, is your best, most real album for over a decade! Write a seven minute no-nothing cock opera! Let Scott Shriner sing! Fuck you!

The *Red Album* concludes the Weezer story, and so that story, then, needs retelling. There are probably in this readership those who did not grow up alongside Cuomo's first two records; there are, we must assume, people for whom the *Blue Album* (1994) did not function as the social metric for the future and *Pinkerton* (1996) the emotional equivalent. You are then innocent of this crime (the *Red Album*'s existence) but will not be spared the punishment (also the *Red Album*'s existence). In the halcyon mid-'90s this small man with funny glasses made simple pop music out of simpler chords and almost asinine words that, somehow, burned like a sun made of empathy, galaxies made of pathos, star clusters mapped liked acne. Was this generational universality unintentional? It appeared so, eventually. Cuomo retired to Harvard, rebuked his masterwork *Pinkerton*, refused the supplication of his person to our collective anxiety. We despaired and got really, really into Modest Mouse, but never forgot about the boy who'd once held us with the innocent omniscient serenity of Kubrick's Starchild.

Into this eager environment came album three, five quiet pubescent years later. Cuomo realized what people "wanted," because he'd spent time exploring the thoughts and feelings of literally billions of people, in at least four time zones, before deciding: fuck those people. Weezer as an institution, Weezer as philosophy, Weezer as a concept fraternized and defiantly not to be fucked with: all this had to go. He purposed a critique, but only said a load of shit about stuff nobody had asked. He gave us riffs we didn't want, he sang in tones we couldn't feel. He pronounced judgment on his own body of work, and then gave us something completely different: a handful of hash boners, an album with a seemly babel of hooks but none of the foreglow.

But right now is the time to reassess the *Green Album* as something Important—and really fucking good! Because it represents the point at which Weezer's existence so-to-speak stopped existing, the big catch-on of which was the immutable power of popular suggestion: *Weezer* (2000)! The letters struck familiar valedictory neurons, as did the vibrations from the speakers. This was Weezer: still Weezer, largely *Weezer* (1994). We listened to those pop songs and maundered their lack of persona. Now we look back and admire it for the same: the guilelessness that let Weezer evaginate from what lay within, that let them move up and out of the ditch, over the turnpike and into the established void of songs about girls and drugs. But these were really good songs! This wasn't *Maladroit* (2002)(which would serve as the guttural middle portion of what now looks like the band's "Suck" trilogy) but just a fast set of inoculated sound, hypercompressed and feverish. It went platinum.

In doing so, it remained supremely and insultingly indifferent. But the *Red Album* is not indifferent. If the *Green Album* marked the disappearance of the band Weezer into itself, the *Red Album* heralds the return with trumpets of fire. The *Red Album* is the point at which indifference charts into the picayune. The *Red Album* makes no "sense," but it offers us an indication of what Weezer might actually "mean." The anonymous trilogy of this decade is over, and the self-loathing trilogy of the last decade has reached its triumphant explosive conclusion. The *Red Album* is Weezer invaginating. The *Red Album* is Weezer coming back into the womb. The *Red Album* is not Blue, or Green or Black, even. It is, like that cover jimmies, one hundred and ten percent Red. This is the real raw meat of Cuomo's craft; it is the soft wet fleshy core of this artistic entity. The *Red Album* is to the Blue one as Milton's Lucifer said to God: "Better to reign in Hell, than serve in Heav'n." This is Rivers growing a dick. This is that dick growing a dick. This is that dick growing a Rivers.

Needless to say, Cuomo is indulging himself here, lavishing the listener with direct ironic/unironic funny/unfunny comments on his own fame and artistic trajectory. But most distressingly, he is indulging us here, too. We longed for this. It's not his increasing age that produced this hideous and deliberate thing, as has been hopefully suggested; it's just him, just as those remarkable, effortless early records were. This is, clearly, what's remarkable about the *Red Album* as well. We now know that the real Cuomo has been this the whole time; he hid from us before but this is the conclusion to the story! The discography makes perfect sense: two separate trilogies, one of Suck and the other three something like Spit. In his endless self-loathing and frustration Cuomo has created an artwork of absolute malevolence. Like Tetsuo at the end of *Akira* (1988), Cuomo's unhappiness, when finally mutated into absolute solipsism, becomes something physical, a fleshy cyberkinetic mass that destroys Neo-Tokyo—or, in this case, destroys the notion of pop music as an agent of anything but self-destruction. Like *Akira*, the *Red Album* equates intellectualism and the artistic impulse with absolute nihilism, but unfortunately the *Red Album* does not have sweet bikes and psychic powers.

What it has is Cuomo—stupid, lonely, self-loathing-and-correct-to-do-so Cuomo. In this light the *Green Album* and corresponding Suck Trilogy seem like acts of mercy, releases of absolute anonymity because he felt this poisonous person emerging from within. How insidiously this beast ingratiates itself! You'd think, first, that this is the best album ever. Except of course it isn't, because "Troublemaker," though fun, is in essence a "Good Life" re-enactment, a conclusion and a re-run so unimaginative that in retrospect it's sort of amazing how Cuomo hasn't delivered the song like this before. The riff ProTools through to lend credence to an argument the band never delivers on. It's good to hear him this playful, to rally on "having seven ke-ods" and tittering at the word "be-otch" like these were the new central questions of his personal catharses. Fucking asshole: Like the following five tracks on this record, to hear it is to forgo relevant critique for a sort of pointed and unambiguous kinship. To be a Weezer fan is to have an ultimately passive-aggressive relationship with a band that only purports to be Weezer, but is really lost in the infinite precision of what that word really means. By explicitly re-hashing old songs and themes ("Heart Songs" = "In The Garage"), Weezer provides us, or them, with a means of deconstructing what had become a depressingly backhanded catalogue.

As such, it is both a strong refutation of every album Weezer has made since *Green* (as it, in its time, seemed to balk at *Pinkerton*) and a numbing confirmation of the only available place this band has left: comic shearing, loose plagiarism, three separate solo projects (all of which are balls). The first six tracks on this record comprise probably the best near-half hour of music this band has produced in a decade. It is festering, garish pop music, too consistent in its absurdity to be ambiguous or interesting, but also too absurd in its consistency to not be (yes) one of the tightest, most enjoyable records to illegally download this year. Whereas before such ruminations would be, well, uninteresting, it now seems merely inappropriate to speculate on the future of this band. Cuomo is fucking nuts. Cuomo is a pop auteur/popular idiot and he probably always envisioned it like this, expanding, finally, in a direction of omni-flatulent largeness, a gross insulting non-expletive, a riff from me to you.

It's difficult to spiritually accommodate further descent from a record that contains the word "boo-yah" along with an earnest, palm-muted nod toward *Nevermind* (1991) along with "Variations on a Shaker Hymn," which in its twinkling starlit grandiosity and glib self-aggrandizement seems to imply both Limp Bizkit and Styx, like some compendium of all that crawls from the earth when God closes his eyes—but, barring natural disaster, this band seems intent upon continuing their scourge of pop music. Elsewhere on the record, Scott Shriner shows up acting like it's okay to just look like that, soft-rock "The Angel And The One" sends shivers down our stupid spines, "Cold Dark World" is obviously inspired by *The Eminem Show* (2002) and Weezer proves, completely and exhaustingly, that music sucks. We have wasted our time, we have wasted yours, because Cuomo has wasted his. Nihilism is the new I-forget-what and liking Weezer is the new hating Weezer. Most art is only a joke without the courage to have a punchline, but here, finally, is the decadent orgasmic fountain of gags Cuomo has been pumping toward for fifteen years. It is ostensibly self-critique, but too trenchant not to implicate us all, too generous in its hate-filled cumspray not to hit even those who never liked the band in the first place, and (though its reach is magnanimous) it inseminates no thing and no one. This is an inverse bukkake, where the ratio of semen wasted to personal shame remains exorbitantly one-sided but where Cuomo is the sole ejaculant and we are the quivering transcendent victims, all transformed through the damning ritual into a slick, febrile mass where everything is the same and yearns to never have been. Ah, music! Ah, spit!

THE HOSPITALS: HAIRDRYER PEACE

Alan Baban
21 July 2008

Hairdryer Peace is like that bit in "Gareth Brown Says" when Falco drops the c-bomb (just six words in!) and things momentarily seem OK/not OK till you realize that this would only be insulting, if it wasn't already so fucking insulting. That's *Hairdryer Peace* (2008) in a nutshell, which, admittedly, I'm being sort of pointless and sort of reductive and sort of really totally fucking missing the point, OK, but I do think you're gonna want to know that this record takes its title (and amazing cover art) pretty seriously. Like, storm samples and everything.

This is a record on some difficult, challenging trip—doing (it seems) pretty much everything over its half-hour to break the listener and push all kinds of tolerance thresholds—and none of it, really, based on noise or mechano-vibration or any of the other reverb-y sleights you'd expect from a band called Hospitals, whose last record (*I've Visited The Island Of Jocks And Jazz* [2005]) seemed to endlessly dwell on the more hostile aspects of its sound. *Hairdryer Peace* is partly like that—it is noisy—but there's nothing trivial or trashy about that noise, and the sorta smugness that can plague scene records has been ushered out for genuine invention.

That said, this is a psychedelic record through and through: taut, and chalked over by soundbites and re-takes and overdubs and the sort of heavy, humidified mixing that centralizes you in on whatever this stuff is without ever really revealing itself. Case in point being the title track and opener: all sliced feedback and barking volume cut so you don't so much hear the bounding drums fade in as feel the skins go straight for the incinerator. And this is before Adam Stonehouse goes on his "I feel queer!" tangent, at which point the thing really goes goose: taking a full swing turn into blues rock territory, except a blues rock built on stray licks and prolapsed introversion loaded with Dylan-baiting and funky keyboard dissonance and the kind of bruised rumination that suggests wasteful existence.

Elements of the mix overlap, and then those overlappings encircle and damn if I've heard another record so insulated, so bent on its own person; like an exacting antithesis of *Weezer* (2008), Peace takes its elements of noise and pushes them to giddy extremes before arranging all the pieces into something aesthetically memorable, and weirdly (weirdly) catchy. There's "Getting out of Bed," which cycles through a surf-rock bass and aggressively panned horns, all blithe to its bedroom juxtaposition, the bubblegum pop of its vocal that weights stoner cadence and finally cedes to what I guess is the sound of tape eating tape. Which is a really good sound and, like the rest of the more "out" elements of Peace, is used sparingly in audacious, genuine what-the-hell moments. "BPPV" takes infolding tubercles of noise and mashes it to horrorhouse keys and mantra drums as Stonehouse slurs and shouts "I feel dizzy / I feel stoked!", like a cartoon character lost in an environment he might have just made himself. "Rules for Being Alive" is a dada take on the talking blues, caught in embryo and situated on some straight borderline between tenderness and something bats. Bum-notes and woozy, oversexed keys move through it like a migraine aura.

The breadth of this record is something special: the breadth of its sound, the fearlessness of its style, the relentless (and winsome) way it wields its own indefinable ambiguity and sets it on constructs not totally there, song-forms that aren't so much open as they're crazily boxed-in and prevented from developing. A lot of *Peace* sounds disorientated (check: "Sour Hawaii") and undifferentiated, but its sounds—the way it recycles its own riffs and fucks with context—retain a sense of direct purpose. Each instrument—and take—seems to fit only insofar as its reach allows; reciprocal identities get smudged and everything, finally, builds to a whole that seems to be witness to its own absence.

So this isn't so much fourteen songs played together fast as it's fourteen tracks so relentlessly and colorfully inventive that it's almost as if this thing we called noise music finally came of a piece; as if these undescended psyche fragments got pulled together by the sheer, swirling momentum of applied trauma and finally congealed into something smooth, consistent, and maybe even frickin' balmy. As a sound map of a uniquely messed-up consciousness, it has the capacity to frighten and puzzle and maybe even mind-alter. More than anything, when (if) it's over, *Hairdryer Peace* feels like it "works." It's a genuinely inspired take on the bedroom wigout.

By the way: you have to hear this thing I did on Goldwave yesterday. It's insane.

FALL OUT BOY: FOLIE A DEUX

Dom Sinacola
12 December 2008

This is a power-pop album released by the biggest Fall Out Boy-ish band working today, on a major label, but it's also 50.4 minutes of Fall Out Boy music—an extended, incomprehensible and surprisingly marketable clamor, ambulance-siren loud, of contradictory signifiers. It is Fall Out Boy as four-headed hermae, guardian of the borders of Fall Out Boy, stentorian, phallic, and unwelcoming. Through *Folie à Deux* (2008) Fall Out Boy both fertilizes and justifies Fall Out Boy, a feat so granite and overwhelming that there is simply no choice left for the listener, the person defined not by aural exposure but by a willingness to explicate Fall Out Boy, but submission.

Yes: catchy. (And also: "Let the guitar scream like a fascist!") But let's be clear: *Folie à Deux*, as with any of Fall Out Boy's increasingly bulbous catalog, acts as a metaphor for playing Fall Out Boy's music, and the music itself is a metaphor for being in Fall Out Boy. Because, lest we forget without repetition, listening to Fall Out Boy's music must somehow be like playing Fall Out Boy's music, so together we're participating in the metaphor of being Fall Out Boy. Fall Out Boy, as we listen to *Folie à Deux*, won't allow us to be anything else but Fall Out Boy, though that involves: tolerance; authority; transition; indecisiveness; a din of ideas without consequence. And being Fall Out Boy is so much more than playing Fall Out Boy's music; being Fall Out Boy is like being my colon(s).

Though I like horns and I like Fall Out Boy, I'm still flummoxed by *Folie à Deux* to the point of admitting Pete Wentz's utter impenetrability. It's exhausting. His lyrics, while phenomenally more lucid than anything to birth from his ilk in ages, are a mess of solipsism (being Fall Out Boy) and assonance (hating Fall Out Boy)—which are both supposed to be fun according to the logic acquired from listening to Fall Out Boy. Then, of course, listening to Fall Out Boy involves adapting to the astounding number of good ideas, totally without focus, that Fall Out Boy cram down each song's gaping maw, and then grinding Lil Wayne into guttural. In Wayne's stead, Fall Out Boy succeeds in shoving Fall Out Boy into our gaping maws, and it feels so right that they do so. I still get goosebumps during the Auto-tuned bridge to "Ashley Blews," but that's only because I can imagine Wentz, Stump, and Weezy mixing it up in the studio. Straight-edge my ass, Pete. I have trouble believing that music so cluttered with longing to be something else could have been made by anyone else than a Pete Wentz and a Fall Out Boy that haven't explored the indulgent breadth of being Fall Out Boy. Fall Out Boy is both made of hellfire and made of cool dudes. And cool dudes do drugs, OK.

By the standards of Fall Out Boy, *Folie à Deux* is a departure from their earlier work but also confident in honing their sound even as they explore venues in sounding like Falco, say, or Billy Joel. Guitars crash in from every conceivable horizon, surrounding poor Falco and poor Billy Joel; "Disloyal Order Of Water Buffaloes" is near perfect Fall Out Boy music, expanded until it fills the universe. By that I mean that Fall Out Boy—either some arsenal of the zeitgeist or a stilling basin for mainstream post-universe—must somehow be the funnest shit I have ever listened to in my life. If it isn't, and "America's Suitehearts" hasn't unleashed some nodal twitter ("What A Catch, Donnie" hasn't made me believe again), then there's no place for me here. I'm quickly, soundly, filled with sadness. I'm alone.

.

MSTRKRFT: FIST OF GOD

Calum Marsh
4 March 2009

FADE IN:

INT. EXPENSIVE AND LUXURIOUS LOFT (NIGHT)

An expensive and luxurious loft, very late at night. It is unclear what
city we are in; could be Seattle or Chicago, but the ratio of women
to men is high and everyone's smoking indoors—come to think of it,
it's probably Montreal. The living room is large and clean. Modern art prints adorn the walls. A high ceiling. Small but powerful
speakers are scattered about the room, tucked here and there behind
potted plants and fish bowls, and from them booms MSTRKRFT's
latest LP, *Fist Of God* (2009).

Album opener "It Ain't Love" fills the air as chic girls in American
Apparel short-shorts and gold lame bras dance around the room,
spilling wine coolers and wiping coke-smears from their upper lips.
The party's DJ—new "On The Go" iPod playlist shuffling away,
his milk crate of vinyl DFA singles unused and ignored on the table
beside his laptop—smooths a crease out of his oversized purple polo
as a wasted 17-year-old slinks by, complimenting his choice of record
as he not-so-subtly admires what lies just beneath her too-transparent
mesh tank-top.

THE DJ

(Tipping his white Yankees cap)
It's the new MSTRKRFT. Part of a little playlist I just whipped up for the party.

17-YEAR-OLD IN TRANSPARENT MESH TANK-TOP
Oh, I love MSTRKRFT! Jessie Keeler is sooo hot.

THE DJ
(To impress)
Yeah, I just downloaded a torrent of the leaked album. Shit is off the hook.

S.Y.O.I.T.M.T-T
Oh, put it on, put it on! I'd just love to hear the whole album.

THE DJ
Uh, well, I just made this whole playlist. It has an obscure remix of "D.A.N.C.E." on it, and…

S.Y.O.I.T.M.T-T
(Touching the DJ's arm, ostensibly to flirt but also to keep balance)
Oh, please. Puh-lease. I'd just love to hear it.

THE DJ
(Smitten)
Oh, alright!

The DJ puts *Fist Of God* on in full and cranks the volume. More dancing commences.

CUT TO:
INT. E. & L. LOFT—KITCHEN

A kitchen off to the side, music volume slightly lower. More hipsters—twentysomethings in royal blue hoodies, oversized plastic sunglasses with neon trim, bottles of Labatt 50 in hands all over the room—scattered about, but considerably less dancing. Sequestered in the corner we find CALUM and his IMAGINARY FRIEND, who only CALUM can see, chatting with one another quietly.

IMAGINARY FRIEND
(Concerned)
You look upset. What's the matter?

CALUM
It's this party. It's irritating.

IMAGINARY FRIEND
You think so? Why?

CALUM
This music is terrible. I abhor MSTRKRFT—I hated their last LP and this sounds even worse. They want to be Daft Punk, and I love Daft Punk, but their records sound so hollow and dull. I don't understand how anyone could be into this.

IMAGINARY FRIEND
But many people are into this. MSTRKRFT have a lot of fans. Look around: people here love this! They're dancing up a storm and I just heard a girl exclaim that this song was "the jam." She also said Jessie Keeler is hot, but she pronounced it as "hawt."

CALUM
The only people who like MSTRKRFT are these samey hipsters. They do lots of coke and read VICE and wear nothing but American

Apparel and listen to shitty music like this.

IMAGINARY FRIEND
Don't be a hypocrite. You shop at American Apparel and you've enjoyed articles in VICE. And really, does it matter what you think of the fans? It should be about the music…

CALUM
But it is about the music! The music is terrible. Listen to this song, "Bounce": "All we do is party / ha ha ha ha." This is the biggest problem with this band and bands like them: too much post-post-post-post anything and everything, all laced with irony and delivered with a winking eye, a nudging elbow. They protect themselves from criticism by refusing to take themselves or their music seriously. It's all so cold and empty and irritating.

IMAGINARY FRIEND
Lighten up—it's just supposed to be fun. You're not supposed to think about it; you're supposed to relax and have a good time.

CALUM
That's what I mean when I say that they protect themselves: any criticism is immediately met with the response that it's "just fun" and that you shouldn't be so serious about it.

IMAGINARY FRIEND
And…

CALUM
… And they're not immune to criticism because they deliver with a smirk. I remember in high school I saw some vapid teen comedy, and when I told my friends that it was terrible they told me that "not

CALUM (con't)
every movie tries to be *Citizen Kane* (1941)." The suggestion being
that anything which is aware of its own vacuity and overall dumbness
is suddenly and completely exempt from any criticism of it being just
that. I refuse to subscribe to that; I'm not going to blindly forgive an
album's problems because it comes with the disclaimer that it isn't
trying to blow your mind and is just meant to be fun.

IMAGINARY FRIEND
So ... you don't like simple fun?

CALUM
Of course I do, but this isn't simple, it's simplistic—there's a difference.

The album comes to "Word Up," featuring Ghostface Killah. No one
seems to know who Ghostface is, somehow, and the party rages on as
normal.

IMAGINARY FRIEND
Okay, but if you have legitimate issues with this record, why are you
bothering with this silly review?

CALUM
You know, my editor was just thinking the same thing ...

IMAGINARY FRIEND
This whole concept review thing is kinda gimmicky, don't you think?
You're just making fun of hipsters, basically.

CALUM
I guess.

IMAGINARY FRIEND
Yet calling you a hipster really wouldn't really be out of the question.

CALUM
...

IMAGINARY FRIEND
Right. So I'm just wondering why you didn't just write a few paragraphs about *Fist Of God*, commenting on its homogeneity and blandness, attacking it for sounding dull and boring and vacuous and so on, rather than writing this script thing, whatever it is, and barely talking about the music on the album at all.

CALUM
...

IMAGINARY FRIEND
And the point of your gimmick, I guess, being that you think hipsters are douchebags—that they like MSTRKRFT and wear similar clothing and do a lot of coke.

CALUM
My point is that MSTRKRFT are terrible and that they will appeal only to coked-out 17-year-old hipsters at house parties who'll listen to anything with a chunky synth and handclaps, and that *Fist Of God* should be avoided by anyone with a discerning ear or shred of taste.

IMAGINARY FRIEND
And so this self-conscious bit at the end here, that's…

CALUM
Uh.

IMAGINARY FRIEND

You protecting yourself from anyone reading this and thinking you're a smug, pretentious douchebag hating on hipsters and MSTRKRFT- without reason, trying to seem … what, clever? Funny? Really?

The album comes to a close and the dancing temporarily subsides as the DJ sifts through his iPod, looking for something else to play. Calum takes a long drink of his bottle of 50 and sighs when he hears the opening blips and bloops of a new Crystal Castles remix. It's going to be a long night.

GHOSTFACE KILLAH: SUPREME CLIENTELE

Clayton Purdom
#2 entry on CMG's Best Albums Of The 2000s list

— 1 —

The other night I had this sequence of dreams so vivid and interrelated as to be narrative: themes and character arcs, specific dialogue volleys, careful scene structure, all framing a loosely supernatural horror story about three men killing a fourth while in the woods. I don't know where it came from; it just emerged fully formed from my sweaty pillow. Things transpired in a sort of timeless cabin, and the woods were Ohioan but bizarre, with whispers of monsters. In the darkness of a nearby barn a centaur pieced together steel for some infernal contraption never seen; he ruled with a quiet authority over the forest's other beasts, the wildest and worst of whom were the three men themselves. In the end he refused to help them and returned to the soldering and smithing of his shadowed machine. I have no idea where this dream came from, and by the time I reached work the next day, I had no idea where it went. The intricacies of the plot disappeared with the night's sweat.

— 2 —

The thing is, I don't really even like *Ironman* (1996). It's not in my top five first-generation Wu-Tang records, after the group debut and solo turns by GZA, Method Man, Raekwon, and ODB. A track like

"Camay," where Ghostface spits at length over a leisurely blunt-burner, shines; elsewhere he feels too eagerly packaged as "the soulful one" for my taste, working mostly as a so-fresh contrast to the nightmarish abstractions of his bedfellows.

But I fucking love *Supreme Clientele* (2000), and always did. It didn't have to be a classic, maybe shouldn't have, logistically, trickling out a few years after "Triumph" stopped banging and into an era of totally lackluster Wu-Tang efforts (*Tical 2000* [1998], anyone?). My first exposure to it was on TV after track practice, flipping between TRL, 106 & Park, and Toonami. It might've been on any of the three that the video for "Apollo Kids" was being debuted. I had never heard rap so grand but so direct before, the beat phasing between the horn blasts I loved on *Moment Of Truth* (1998) and the string-laden theatricality of *Internal Affairs* (1999). The video was all shoes and industrial surfaces, and while I had no idea what the fuck this mink-stoled man was saying I heard in him a confluence of the staggering cockiness I found in Jay-Z and Eminem and the dense, intellectual musicality that made the Roots' "You Got Me" and Black Star's "Respiration" two of my then-favorite tracks. It was somehow both more rambunctious and more sublime than all of that, though, as wild as any of the punk-rock I was still shearing off my CD collection, but decidedly—almost aggressively—hip-hop.

Three years later, I'm a freshman in college—listening, at this point in my life, exclusively to Wu-Tang's first record. I start to piece in the solo records from my roommate's collection, eventually picking up a used copy of *Supreme Clientele* for five bucks from a used record store uptown. The record sprawled, befuddled, banged infinitely. I would think the track was skipping, and then Ghostface would start rapping over it. I'd think there was a hook, and it'd be a half-assed outro. On "One" the beat became part of the raps; on "Woodrow the

Base Head" a skit boasted the quotability and huge drops of a single. Whenever I dug into the lyrics I came away more confused than I was before, eventually discerning that here was an entire recalibration from the old Wu-Tang language bases of five-percenter mythology, kung-fu flicks, and New York name-checking. That code I had worked hard to decipher didn't get me in here. At some point, I got sidetracked from its intrigue.

I have since grappled mightily with the emcee's output. On a personal list, *The Pretty Toney LP* (2004) made my #11 spot of the decade—with *Purple Haze* (2004), it explores a post-*Blueprint* (2001) idea of mainstream rap as a forum for wildly idiosyncratic self-actualization, something Wayne would later take a lot from. But I've decried at probably too many opportunities the goony self-caricature created on Ghostface's four records thereafter. He is an increasingly sour emcee, trafficking in bogus and mostly boring stories about cumshots and stick-ups, getaways and whoopsy-daisies. Nothing has diminished my affection for *Supreme Clientele*, but the harsh, ugly cocaine fetishism that has come to dominate his ouevre only looks less and less interesting when compared to the earlier triumph. At times they seem to be the work of a different person altogether.

– 3 –

This one time, in a flash, I thought I was "getting" *Supreme Clientele*. Like, completely. The logic worked, the stories and reference points made sense—clearly, a lot of drugs were involved. I had just moved to Chicago and was working in a shitty upscale restaurant full of miserable people at the time, feeling generally bad about everything, and working day-after-day to get through *Ulysses* (1922) as if conquering chapters of that might lend a steady measuring stick for the days that rushed unchecked by me. In a fit, I ingested a pile of drugs one night, and at peak their properties were hallucinogenic. When Ghostface announced into a hush that this rap was like ziti I stood in the canyon into which his words fell, and when they crashed high-speed into "strawberry kiwi" that canyon turned Technicolor. Or was this a getaway vehicle? I had found, like Stuart Gilbert's essential study of *Ulysses*, the skeleton key: the code that had eluded me. I thought about writing it down while I floated around my pitch-black bedroom that night, thought about grabbing these principles from the air and committing them to paper but of course did not and of course as soon as I woke up the next day and as the night's residue drip-dried off my spinal cord so too went that essential understanding I had reached with the album the previous night. At first I still saw the shapes, but then even the shapes faded. I remember now only a feeling of certainty as I bobbed around my kaleidoscopically hot apartment that night, followed by a particularly rough shift at the restaurant the next day.

– 4 –

There is a lot of insecurity for some people when listening to rap music, in that much of it is very coded or low-brow or both. Something like, say, OJ Da Juiceman requires a good deal of foreknowledge to properly enjoy, and while the infamously inscrutable *Supreme Clientele* seems like the epitome of this it is the exact opposite. It sits atop this list (rap-wise) because it is a great leveller. You don't need to know about New York or Wu-Tang or Mathematics or even mathematics to get this record, because you're not going to get this record. Even its tracklisting and liner notes are skewed to obfuscate. Like *Kid A* (2000), which a lot of people think should top a list such as this, it is unfeelingly abstruse, and so somehow a reflection of this era; unlike that record, it is a whole lot of fun. It is still a Friday night rap record, soulful and body-moving and funny.

If I had to describe *Supreme Clientele* in a phrase, then, it would be as a syntactical playground, where individual words don't matter so much as the way Ghostface darts between them. But a larger metaphor may also be in order. Pushed out as these words are by the thousand here their array takes on the feel of a star chart, with individual lines serving as constellations drawn among them. Thus the English language is treated as the cosmos—Joyce's "heaventree of stars hung with humid nightblue fruit"—and we sit as kids on a clear night marveling at their density, their beauty, their luminosity and age. The simplest of these shapes pulled from the sky involves the brightest stars, like when on "One" Ghost pulls a line from the North Star to his very neighborhood, spitting at a mic-trembling holler, "The Devil planted fear inside the black babies / Fifty cent sodas in the hood, they going crazy." On a track like "Nutmeg" the diversity of effect is closer to a laser light show: "Olsive compulsive lies flies with my name on it / Dick made the cover now count, how many veins on it / Scooby snack jurassic plastic gas booby trap," and on breathlessly forward. Elsewhere he subsumes whole verses from Rakim and Divine Force, but the words seem like his, too: memories, older shapes traced in the sky as the linguistic display stretches into its second half, turning ramshackle and various. The topics may remain fuck-you or fuck-her or whatever else but on *Supreme Clientele* rap's common tropes are a means to an end, a telescope that brings our eyes closer to the sky. What we are actually seeing is much older than rap, although—composed as it is of stars—this shit is still as hot as the sun.

Because '00s rap had only to challenge what came before it, crystalline as *Ready to Die* (1994) and *The Low End Theory* (1991) and *Aquemini* (1998) were. Badu used its elements as the tools for a '70s-worthy soul album, Jay-Z and Kanye doggedly pursued its synthesis with pop music, Cannibal Ox and the Clipse found the genre's common lineage with experimental and electronic production—but *Supreme Clientele*, atop them all on this list, is defiantly hip-hop. Just hip-hop, rather: just sad guitar and soul samples, well-chopped drums, just dudes rapping and occasionally singing. Ungilded, opaque: hip-hop, street raps. The skit "Who Would You Fuck" is exactly what it sounds like. That it knocks hard front to back—"Wu Banga 101" arrives at track 18 of 20—isn't the point, because every rap album on this list does. There is, obviously, something else at play here, to have reached across the staff's many tastes (only some rap-centric) to land here, second only to an album that contains all our tastes at once. *Supreme Clientele* is completely hip-hop, but it is also bigger than hip-hop.

And—queue Dead Prez beat—what's bigger than that?

– 5 –

My dream the other night was something, I don't know what. It felt more substantial than my typical flights of fancy, which have grown infrequent as I've gotten older, or my typical dreams, which are uninteresting assemblages of professional anxiety and half-remembered relationships. I believe if captured accurately though the dream's story would've been one I want to tell, conveying truths I deeply believe (that humans can't outgrow their animalistic nature) in an aesthetic that resonates with me (that is, horror). But I'm not a fiction guy—I let it slide, wrote a concert review instead. My point is not that I am special, or that that dream was special. My point is that while I don't know if there is a God I do know that story didn't come from me, fully formed and complete of itself, and that wherever such a dream came from—a rush of inspiration shooting through my neural channels and coming out in a manner unique to my tastes—is bigger than me. Bigger, as it were, than hip-hop.

What resonates with listeners about *Supreme Clientele* is the sound of a man animated fully by this lightning—composed of it, his voice trebly with electricity, explaining the contours of each electric flash in the language that works for him, the stories that work for him. He'd tell those stories again later but not suffused with such wild and joyous inspiration, sounding not so much struck with inspiration as in complete communion with it. The record is a singular triumph, but it is also an individual one: Ghost's alone. The rabble of producers, label interference, Wu backstory, even his own discography stretching out before and after this point can't obscure the shock of breathless emceeing here. Nor can the dazzle of its competition to reach this place, nor can the reams of singles that have truly defined this genre this decade. "Stay Fly" can't beat this. "B.O.B." can't beat this. Hova man-king can't beat this, Can Ox can't beat this. It is the triumph of one person—of one mic. In that capacity it fulfills hip-hop's promise as a forum for artistic excellence among the systemically forgotten. With *Illmatic*, it is the most remarkable album-length performance by an emcee ever recorded.

THE AVALANCHES: SINCE I LEFT YOU

Mark Abraham
#1 entry on CMG's Best Albums Of The 2000s list

SILY slyly asks, "can you think of anything else that talks, other than a person?", and answers "a record," as if it itself can talk. Silly, right? Or serious? Because *SILY* sort of asks this all-important question importantly by proxy, sort of. It's vocalized second hand, but is not second hand in its vocalization; it's just a sample of what you may already be thinking. It's your voice, I mean; you're asking—obviously, since we've all asked this—"why does this album talk to me?" While you ponder, Suzy also wonders who is looking at her; champagne gets poured; people get on planes; people party; the joint gets turned upside down, featuring a whole lot of flutes; tonight may have to last you your entire life. That's the text—this is a party record; a hip-hop record; a breaks record—and the way this album gets talked about you would think listening to it would be like ingesting Ibiza. Ingesting the sun, even. Somebody probably wishes the word "balearic" had been invented in 2000. And maybe I'll get 2000 emails for that factual inaccuracy, one for every year of the 2000 years previous to the one when this thing dropped. Those very sad 2000 years, I mean.

Because *Since I Left You* (2000) isn't a culmination, or an anticipation; this is a cusp, a wormhole. It's everything second hand, lit up in first person, sped up to the point where everything is blurred, since it never left us with anything but things we love. In 2000, it was a manifesto (intentionally or unintentionally) for a decade that hadn't happened yet: a world so new. This is promise in its purest form. "Can't you hear it?" But it's also a funnel, where the second hands cup together to funnel us from the 1990s to the 2000s. I just got to that part in "Electricity" where future M83 gives way to past *The Chronic* (1992) and then they play in tandem, like they're in love. "Some birds are funny when they talk." Do you think Dan Snaith listened to "Extra Kings" before making *Up in Flames* (2003)? Isn't "Radio" just better than most of the DFA catalogue anyway? Isn't "A Different Feeling" blueprinted off the rhythms of a tiger's orgasm? Is it that epic, or is it just a band having fun? Does it matter? There's enough mythology; I like this album way better than *Endtroducing...* (1996); I'm not the one to talk about how sick the process of collage is here. I mean, I actually probably am, but I won't. Neither will I quote Bismarck about sausages. I'll just hint at the quote, since this album doesn't succeed by being literal anyway, Girl Talk. Since I Left You blurs; you're just blurry. You're just "an ophthalmologist" with "juice on your chin." They're the "Frontier Psychiatrist." A real frontier; a place where everything is possible. Even sampling what I'm pretty sure is an Anthony Banks synthesized string riff from *We Can't Dance* (1991). The frontier is always a collage, where the new and the second hand meet.

Also second hand, in the sense that means "abandoned" or "left behind"—"pre-loved"—was an erroneous piece of mail that arrived at my Toronto home last week. It was for nobody who lives here; it was for everybody, therefore. Just like this album. There are three apartments and a restaurant here; none of us listen to the same music, but thanks to albums like this we all kind of do, whether because when I blare this in our kitchen and I wander to another room for a moment I can hear "Flight Tonight" thrumming through the walls like a bumping party downstairs or because this album is every music anyway. I was making carrot cake when I realized that. I put bourbon in my cream cheese icing to make it less cheesy; the Avalanches somehow strike the same balance and avoid a slight half-step left to cheese-stache purgatory. They left the right way, I mean: this is an album that samples Madonna and that band with that song with that chorus with that line, "Oh Annie / I'm not you're Daddy / But if I were you wouldn't be so ugly." And with that, I dedicate this blurb to Annie, because as groovy as they were, Kid Creole and the Coconut Gang were kind of douchey. Kid Creole should be the recipient of this week's bonus Band Name Anagram: a "canal shave."

Scratch that. I'm going to dedicate this blurb to Leah—who I love despite the fact that we do and don't love the same music; who I can live with because we both listen to every music anyway—who once demonstrated in the most poignant way exactly how the samples on this album work. Normally, Leah won't eat unethically raised meat. She's very strict about this, except when she's drunk, and she suddenly really wants Chicken McNuggets. She even has a little song that she sings to me about sweet and sour dipping sauce. But sometimes you just want Chicken McNuggets, right? No matter how suspect their production/cred/creation was or is. Sometimes you just want sweet and sour. This record is both, thankfully. And with 3500 samples, that's like 3500 bursts of either. Some are sharp and some blunt, but they turn the joint upside down. They leave juice on your chin. Sweet and exotic, but not foreign. This album doesn't play that game. Maybe a kumquat? Can't you hear it? Check that really slow part on "Etoh" that sounds like the beginning of an awesome Animal Collective song 4 years early, before somehow the band manages to distinctly capture an impression of dancehall and afro-beat playing simultaneously, before "Summer Crane" yé-yés its arrival on a breath of Steve Reich vocalization, before that Genesis quote. And that's without mentioning that "Summer Crane" sounds like Gang Gang Dance. That's two songs. This album, in the most literal way possible, links all of our spines together to form a staircase that reaches the heavens. It's a bunch of dominoes that fall into one another. It blurs the lines between creating and collage; it acknowledges what our entire lives are anyway: a collage of ideas folded into one another.

And so I folded the wrongly-addressed letter into a summer crane. It was addressed to a person named Vance Ernst. Possibly he's Annie's brother, or son, or daughter; across generations we tell stories that draw us all together anyway. Maybe he's the daddy; maybe he thinks he's a Daddy O; maybe he's the guy who created Chicken McNuggets. Themselves a collage, really. The letter was from a gym; the address was an apartment that doesn't exist in this building; the name sounds fake anyway. "Vance Ernst." I mean, come on: Vance Ernst is a joke. Vance is also a collage; he is all of us. Vance Ernst dreams of going to the gym so that when music like this plays his body is always ready: taut, sharp, and thick. It is music that demands you be ready. Booming. In this, Vance is better prepared than me. I can only offer carrot cake and a beard full of past carrot cakes. And the internet, since even with all the every music I listen to, I don't always know what's happening on this album. Like, so many flutes and not one Bobbie Humphrey sample? Who picked this for our album of the year? Is that the question you're asking? I couldn't hear; I'm at that part in "Pablo's Cruise" that sounds like a Philip Jeck joint. Does "Spockily" mean "as Spock would do it?" Because with everything I'm saying, there's also just how fucking good this shit is.

The secret—and maybe Vance knows it—is that the stray bits are vaguely familiar but never recognizable. Was this blurb hard to read? Did it make you hungry for carrot cake? Stray bits and pieces and ideas reformed as unfurled sails that propel shit forward. Cosmic shit, I mean, wrapped in nautical imagery. Hell, even the artwork is specific, but then cropped to become unspecific, new, and meaningful. A painting of a ship sinking becomes a painting of different boats with just one fluctuating wave caught between them. Point being, *Since I Left You* isn't silly or second-hand at all. It is unrepentantly immediate. Its ground always shifts; it is a frontier. An album from 2000 can be The Album Of The 2000s because it is the future built of the past. I mean, repetition is what repenting is, right? *Since I Left You* is like a millennial rosary chain, a history textbook with no course to assess you, ideas refashioned to a collage that is blurred enough that it loses any sense of collageness. Which is why even though I'm sure Vance and I have nothing in common, this album is both of our albums of the decade because this album makes me and Vance the same: defined as undefinable, a unique whole built from repetitive parts, and pretty awesome besides. Come on: nothing talks like *Since I Left You*, and it talks to you because it talks like everything.

INTERLUDE:
SITE SLOGANS, 2005-2010

Staff

Editor's Note: At some point we decided to include a slogan on the site each week. This was possibly an attempt at branding, but within, say, one week, it turned into a place to post gnomic and generally offensive phrases culled from the staff messageboard. When we redesigned the site in 2010, we scuppered the sloganhole, thinking they'd go to Twitter instead (they did not). Some of our less shameful but still deeply shameful slogans are preserved below, in the interest of historical honesty.

"We're not competent, but we're terrific"

"We're Mike Jones."

"Over 10,000 Seth Cohens Served."

"Fuck my review on there."

"Expect the Best, Accept the Worst."

"Because we're not smart enough to write books."

"Maladroit sucks."

"The Porky's of music criticism."

"Because if we don't talk about us, who will?"

"Sorry, Grandma."

"Competence is our Costume."

"Your fact-checkin cuz."

"If we had a good one, we wouldn't be having a slogan contest."

"It's really annoying when people talk about Peter Hepburn at my school."

"We've ruined Christmas."

"Slate reads us."

"Obviously not in your time zone."

"Hey speaking of clowns..."

"No seriously way to go Canada"

"I'll raise you a Terry Bozzio"

"and by the hives i mean wu-tang"

"see i hate that. we are very different types of linkin park fans."

"there will be parties (/blood)"

"I've been avoiding it for so long, but "the Steely Dan thing" is happening to me."

"F my 100 percents would be like throwing roses at a sunset"

"I donno about those mild lyrics and tobacco reference though."

"I spy a Literature dropout with erectile dysfunction."

"I know everyone is into everything and don't make assumptions and stuff"

"6th form wanky turgid bollocks"

"Slo ho ho ho hogan"

"How are the '09 coffins shaping up?"

"He seems like the worst dude ever and I resent his success"

"its amazing that it took them around 15 years to come up with "Mistress for Christmas" as a song title."

"I once licked a toad in Bolivia and woke up in the jungle three years later"

"halo 3 is a fucking sport. it's art when i play it, though."

"I stood on my kitchen table and did Tai Chi to this last night."

"because Leos are lions and lions COME FROM AFRICA."

"this reminds me to find a copy of that one mary j blige album i always liked."

"Turns out the internet is only, like, seven meters across"

"saturday accomplished."

"i just saw big jumping cellphones, got confused and moved on"

", come the fuck on"

"I let out a long, mournful fart this morning and it's name was Beeeeeeeeejaaaaaaaarrrrr"

"It's been that kind of month/year/life."

"a shithouse of cynicism"

"I worship at the awesome church of Grace Jones/Joan Collins Orthodox Awesomeness."

"it stirs up anger problems in me I didn't know existed"

"human interaction is so fucked this year"

"my money's on the inside of my eyelids."

"it was a really special event. i'd never seen anything like it offline."

"I'm drunk with confidence and primed for bad decisions."

"holy fuck do i have the shits today"

"Sixtoo discredits us."

"What the hell have you done with Betz?"

"Oh, njø we di'in"

"Also, codeine is not the solution."

"No Clayton, we never reached that consensus"

"You're not the first to equate clumsily chosen, faux erudite words equalling insight."

"I'm still young enough for a trendy indie rock soundtrack and well-shot traffic scenes to be evocative"

"you can do whatever you desire to michael cera ... with words"

"I'm your elder, respect my fists."

"you're doing a funny impression of nonsense."

"How incredibly sad is it that I know what Chris Issak's drummer looks like?"

"It's okay. I put an extra long free improv piece in my podcast to help you sooth your nerves."

"on top of that, swordfigthing to Knights of Cydonia."

"Pisces Iscariot, which my dad is inexplicably really into"

"passed out as in tired as fuck, not as in i'm letting him bleed out on the floor while i edit a Primal Scream review"

"we need more music reviews that are a picture of me, wide-eyed on a mountaintop cumming in my pants while wearing headphones"

"Just shut up and air guitar to it, Chomsky."

"See, funny pictures of Mike Love looking like a douche make people laugh. Pictures of pug dogs don't."

"Whoa, you speak Latin?"

"it's time to pick the ephedrines from the ephrodiums."

"Fuck Off, Cokemachineglow"

"Shut up Conrad."

"live for the choogle and die for the choogle."

"the uk seems to suck at discernment, which is just not right. we are class."

"hey, tape hiss and drone are people, too."

"so that's what friendship looks like."

"this marshmallowy development to your writing style can only get more interesting."

"If you wanna come check out this cold sore I have on my lip, call my cell"

"Again, the public servants thing. Go to hell, readers."

"way to fucking go, alphabet"

"awesome. hippies, though."

"The internet is a series of tubes, right?"

FROG EYES:
PAUL'S TOMB: A TRIUMPH

Chet Betz & Dom Sinacola
8 May 2010

In *Paul's Tomb* (2010) we dream the dreams of Frog Eyes and we share, trembling, in their nightmares. That is: where once the winding progressions of past Frog Eyes songs were like watching churlish waves and wondering what's causing them and what will happen—because surely there is something mighty at play and something mighty in store—here we are cast right into that frothing ocean. Or at least so goes the perspective of the newly converted. For those of us who've been entrenched in this ongoing saga that is Frog Eyes' reluctant stagger towards entelechy, *Paul's Tomb* acts like anything Carey Mercer tends to create—breathlessly, maddeningly, with a soft, wet heart and a cinderblock head. That is: the intimation of drowning is palpable, is heavy and very real; Frog Eyes, at the crown of which Mercer seems to embody the very essence of his band's name, is holding onto the listener for dear life. We still may not fully understand, almost ten years since we first began not to understand, but still this music makes sense in the sense that we can't help but feel this music for how visceral it is and how the unpredictable roll of its crests and dips can only be taken as inevitable and unyielding.

As a guitar record *Paul's Tomb* may be, somewhat surprisingly, the best guitar record since, gosh, *Pink* (2005)? We should probably just put it aside of any Boris record because these guitars aren't about force so much as persuasion. They're having an impassioned conversation, a conversation about Mercer's lyrics, and they are having the only truly insightful conversation on that topic because their language is erudite rock music, their breath is their unique phrasing, and their gestures a fairly dazzling myriad of textures (check about a minute into "Lear in Love" where it sounds like the Walkmen hopped into the studio, spent an hour setting up their instruments, and did a ten-second one-take) as assisted by accomplished producer Daryl Smith. So the low-end's a little soupy, so what: the adept accompaniment of Melanie Campbell's drums and Megan Boddy's keys seem unaware of anything else besides those guitars, the guitars seemingly unaware of anything else besides the clouds boiling out of Mercer's ears. If there's a role-switch anywhere it'd be on "Odessa's War" when the drums are the only ones to follow Mercer into his climax (that's husband and wife at work), and if there's an exception that proves the rule it'd be the lite-on-guitar "Violent Psalms," which sounds almost as if Mercer and a girl are doing a cappella even though they're totally not. Because without those iconic guitars to frame the picture, Mercer's chiaroscuro takes up and even overflows the screen.

"Violent Psalms" is also where we're most clearly introduced to new band addition Boddy, her voice Mercer's album-long temperance and what might as well be the synthesis of all this record's female characters. She could be Judith with decapitated head held aloft or Cassandra standing before the Trojan Horse, only slightly comforted in her correctness, or together the distillation of their calm, seething power. More importantly, in some wispy form or another she's already been Mercer's Donna, the unobtainable muse of his 2009 solo album, *Skin Of Evil*. It is here that Boddy inhales all the voices that aren't Mercer's so as to let out a single, soothing counterpart to everything brash and ragged and crumbling and doubtful in Mercer's milieu. That "Violent Psalms," in its spare respite from everything else the album's been spewing, sounds like a *Skin of Evil* B-side should make ineffable sense—in the sense that we can't help but draw circulatory, sprawling skeins from one Mercer track to another.

This is, after all, a Frog Eyes album made of Frog Eyes songs, and Frog Eyes songs are inextricable from their songwriter. As is Mercer's wont, he's collected the skeletons of what he's played with ruthlessly before, the bones mostly cast loosely into the dark so all these old motifs and recycled themes clang about loudly, leaving big, creepy echoes throughout. It's obvious what he's doing—at least if, having followed Mercer's career up to this point, so much about *Paul's Tomb* seems deeply familiar. The Donna of "Styled By Dr. Roberts" can only be Mercer's Donna, who will always be Mercer's Donna, and if that name isn't imprinted legibly enough on Mercer's forehead, "Dr. Roberts" culls a striking line from the previously mentioned solo outing, flips it, and answers the lament he sighed almost a year ago. "I see my life is made of rain," he once wailed; here he wails back, "I see my life isn't made of rain," and whether that's a good thing or not is lost to the song's awe-struck conclusion. For it's not to be taken lightly that the subtitle of this record is "A Triumph," and there are several moments where Mercer's narrator(s)—Joyce would be proud—encounter what may be a divine light emanating from Beatrice-like muses. Amidst that resonant slow-mo at the end of "Dr. Roberts" Mercer cries, "And if you love me / You'll know my heart belongs to the shepherd / Who has nursed his lord back from the tombs of a dark Galilee" before boldly jumping right into the idea that the only tangible expression or experience of Christ is to love someone else (later in "Paul's Tomb" equating anything resembling a crusade with a mockery of faith and in fact threaded into "the misery of Christ") and he will know who that someone is by the "light streaming off of [her] face," the once sonorous drums halting before that vision. While ravishing in its simplicity, the moment's made even more pleasurable by realizing the scope of this emotion Mercer's launched parabolically from one album to another, incandescent insignia streaking the smoke-filled mid-afternoon. So it's an earned arbor when on the next song, "Lear In Love," Mercer repeatedly asserts, "I kissed a girl / She was the only one who seemed to hold on to the shards of light" (as opposed to cherry chapstick). This makes things "all right." At least until "Violent Psalms" carries forth the last down-note of "Lear in Love" into its dirge about depressed silhouettes and oil baths.

On Spinner.com Mercer talks about this record being "liminal" and as one listens to the conflict here between certainty of life and certainty of death it begins to sound a bit like Mercer's coloring in the void between testaments old and new with a post-Renaissance, post-modern palette and doing so in a way that jolts us around between different viewpoints and settings and maybe even narrative realities like so much *Lost* season 6. It's in this whirlpool context that romantic faith and nihilistic doubt are streamed downward together towards a pit leading either to nothingness or some glorious "Cloud Of Unknowing." Thus, from "Violent Psalms" we have "Paul is alive, Paul is alive" (the apostle?) quickly put in check by "on and on, the Great Debaser" (Time?) and then in the very next song a claim is made that Paul is "never gonna break on through." Can anything conclusive be said about the fact that in the dying moments of "Violent Psalms" we have a synth repeating what sounds like the first line of the melody to "This Is My Father's World"? Which then in turn only brings us to the wealth of father issues inherent to Mercer's work, as mentioned in our review of *Tears of the Valedictorian* (2007), illustrated here in a sovereign love that for one reason or another is made unavailable ("but you know, you just can't have it") or pretends that it's undesired, its all-too-present counterpart the manifestations of an abusive patriarchy. Is God a deadbeat dad or are these particular children just too lost? Are all these muses at the mercy of a corrupt world and a Dark Lord ("a hurter") who will not fail in destroying them, or will their light somehow persist? It seems the best thing to do is simply let the contradictions render each other blameless, the contrast stark and absolute. And listen to the awesome guitars. Which bring us back to Mercer's aching howl, carrying with it that tome of sacred protest. The hook digs deeper.

The very accessibility of Mercer's nostalgia—of his characters and salvos and melodies and voices—is Mercer's admission that he's still not quite finished. Which is funny, because Frog Eyes songs have always felt slightly unfinished, like they were let go in their pubescence and told to fight it out in the yard for the last marshmallow. How exciting, Mercer seems to be telling us, to witness this music tussle with itself until it finds a balance, an equilibrium—some sort of stable in-between. In the final, title track the tempo decelerates through a series of brilliant crescendos, bringing us at last to the record's end, a swell of instruments finishing themselves off much the way Mercer finishes off the hopes of his characters trapped in a savior-less paradigm. You could say it's a chilling moment but it'd be more apt to say it's the last violent shudder eked out at the end of the entire album's long, arduous shiver. But, again, *Paul's Tomb* is "a triumph," right? What Frog Eyes suggests, then, ferociously and unforgettably, is that it does not matter what that triumph is in a hypothetical way. It only matters in what that triumph represents now, the band with their wrists shackled "to that razor-like rim." This record truly is a triumph, and it allows itself to be an open-ended one because this is how it goes on and on, on and on, matching step with the Great Debaser—hell, waltzing with the motherfucker. Donna is alive.

LCD SOUNDSYSTEM: THIS IS HAPPENING

Mark Abraham
19 May 2010

I'm going to poke fun at Pitchfork just a bit, but only because their opinion on LCD Soundsystem's *This Is Happening* (2010) is probably the standard by which all other opinions of the album will be judged. I'm not even sure, given the endless "Pitchfork Hearts LCD Soundsystem" publicity blitz we've been subjected to so far this year, that it's possible to have an opinion about This that doesn't necessarily confirm or deny their 9.2 rating that suggests LCD Soundsystem is more or less exactly as good as James Murphy has always been, which is 0.8 away from being perfect. But since they've now slapped an identical rating on both the second and third LCD Soundsystem LPs let me try to explain my reasoning. Think about it: we learned today that in Pitchfork's view, *This* and *Sound Of Silver* (2007) are both apparently almost as good as *Exile On Main Street* (1972), but the reason This is explained to be that good is little more than hand waving that takes the form of repeated hints that Murphy is essentially our generation's David Bowie. Which…okay, but you'll have to forgive me for thinking this argument is an attempt to solve the difference between apples and oranges by saying, "oranges are just like apples and remember when apples were cool?" It's not like I think David Bowie is some sacred cow; I just don't get the comparison, starting with the fact that I can tell you the difference between *Hunky Dory* (1971) and *Scary Monsters (And Super Creeps)* (1980) and the other nine albums (!) Bowie released between 1971 and

1980 but I can only really tell you what's consistent between *LCD Soundsystem* (2005), *Sound Of Silver*, and *This*.

More importantly, even if we accept rickety parallels between the two artists, Murphy echoing Bowie doesn't lend any actual weight to This as an album, just as Pitchfork's recent attempts to characterize Broken Social Scene as an epic clash of egos and dreams in the vein of … well, I assume Fleetwood Mac, though they don't say this out-right, or to tease out the similarities between the career arcs of Joanna Newsom and Joni Mitchell? None of these parallels, even if we accept that they exist, have any meaning beyond reductively characterizing bands and artists that we care about in the present by hinging their relevance on things we understand from the past. Which seems to me to be kind of backwards. And further, in the specific case of This, neither does the implication that Murphy styles his sonic palette the way Bowie did in the late 1970s carry water: there's a huge difference between Brian Eno walking into a Berlin studio and enthusiastically playing Donna Summer's "I Feel Love" (1977) for Bowie—i.e. mak-ing rock music that appreciates broader musical trends—and James Murphy hearing Daft Punk and thinking, "I should make a song that sounds like Daft Punk, that mentions Daft Punk, and that verifies that yes, indeed, I'm a fan of Daft Punk." Neither is wrong, or less valuable; it's just the difference between showing and telling. It's the difference, as I suggested in our Top 100 Albums of the Decade list, between the Avalanches and Girl Talk. When This single "Pow Pow" was released, tell me your first thought wasn't "this sounds like Talking Heads." And even if we're being more nuanced: "this sounds like Talking Heads mixed with Lizzy Mercier Decloux, some overtly gothic vocal runs, and some ESG on the low end." Which is pretty par for the course at this point, isn't it? Especially the part where Murphy has yet to recapture the magic resulting from a similar cen-trifuge of styles when producing his masterful "Yeah" 12" (2004).

The second contextual aspect to Pitchfork's appraisal of Murphy's career places *This* as a culmination of his experiments to transform his post-punk influences into dance tracks. But again I'm stuck: I'm not sure when Pitchfork decided that Murphy was suitable shorthand for the post- and dance-punk revival of the first half of the last decade that also featured a whole bunch of other, equally interesting and talented bands, many of which still exist. Is it just because the easiest way to deal with the *Echoes* (2003) fuck-up is to give all the props to the man behind the curtain? That's an easy joke, I know, but giving Murphy all this praise seems like another hand wave that shoos away the relevance of, just to name obviously PF-approved bands, the Fire Show, Mu, Hot Hot Heat, Bloc Party, Love is All, Franz Ferdinand, !!!, Ladytron, Death from Above 1979, Annie, Robyn, Liars, Enon, the Long Blondes, O.U.T.H.U.D., Tom Vek, Yeah Yeah Yeahs, or any number of other bands and artists central to the re-figuring out of how to turn punk music into something you might dance to. Ultimately, that seems just as weird to me as opting to fit Murphy in with Bowie over bands to which he clearly owes his ancestry: ESG and Liquid Liquid, obviously, but also the Au Pairs, Danielle Dax, Y-Pants, the Associates, Delta 5, P-Model, Chrome, Dead Can Dance, Gang of Four, Killing Joke, Lene Lovich, Decloux, Orchestral Maneuvers in the Dark, Prefab Sprout, Soft Boys, Yazoo, Scritti Politti, Cyndi Lauper, Madonna, R.E.M., Talking Heads, U2, blah blah blah. Point being, shoving Murphy into the Bowie box doesn't make sense as anything but an attempt to paint Murphy with the strokes of Bowie's relevance. Or maybe "Heroes" (1977)—which, admittedly, Murphy tries his hardest to get "All I Want" to sound like—is just a hipper touchstone than "Telegraph" (1983)—which is what "All I Want" actually sounds like—because Orchestral Maneuvers In The Dark were on the *Pretty In Pink* soundtrack (1986)?

I really think This needs to be removed from that context to have any sort of useful discussion about it. See, the members of the Cokemachineglow staff do not all agree on the relative quality of this album (nor, to be fair, do I assume that the entire Pitchfork staff feels the same way about it). The one thing we all do agree on, however, is that there's nothing epic about This. The staunchest defenders of the record in our ranks are not of the "Murphy is misunderstood and put upon and this rocks and you're too uptight to like it" school; they're simply talking maybe a high 70 score, and they're basing that on this old chestnut: it's a well-made fun album, so who cares if Murphy is a dick or his lyrics suck? Well … I have little to say about those lyrics in a specific sense that doesn't simply repeat analysis Conrad has already masterfully provided in his previous engagements with LCD Soundsystem, but I do think it's worth stepping back for a second to appreciate just why I'm not sure I buy the argument that Murphy's lyricism is irrelevant. Besides, you know, the fact that Murphy is bad at writing lyrics.

Like, I don't actually think James Murphy is a dick. I think he's obscenely self-aware that he has a dick, as is the male-dominated music media that loves him, but mostly I'd suggest that the problem isn't dickishness so much as the way he's kind of hilariously hamstrung by being granted this weird guru-ish position by Pitchfork and other media outlets to playfully explore concepts of hipness and irony and aging masculinity and whatever else has become his current bugaboo, as if he has total authority on the subject. He gets this pass because he's held up, explicitly or implicitly, as an example of how millennial indie rockness—literally, how having fun—doesn't have to die when you turn 40 (as he now has), or have kids, or get married, or whatever. The problem, as horrible ideas like This's lead single "Drunk Girls" make abundantly clear, is that Murphy's world view—at least as he often clumsily expresses it in his music—doesn't seem particularly deep, leading him to stumble whenever he tackles subjects that have the potential to make him look like a dick. Which does kind of make him a dick, but also kind of an unwitting dick. At some point, playing at having a *Maxim* worldview and having a *Maxim* worldview melt into one another, and I can't tell the difference, and I especially can't tell the difference with Murphy because, again, he is bad at writing lyrics.

See, he can get away with the simple and un-deep sentiment of "All My Friends," which explores personal anxieties about getting older and how life affects friendship, or This's "I Can Change," which explores the effects being in love has on one's individuality, because both songs seem sincere enough that his shit doesn't get weighed down by his inability to differentiate between himself and his satire of himself—even if I have to ask what's quite so appealing about a life philosophy that is constantly lamenting all the ways an individual has to change to accommodate their relationships with other people. But songs like "Drunk Girls" and "Pow Pow"? If you don't want folks to smart at you for careless bluster, you probably shouldn't—in the otherwise cute "I Can Change"—gender "love" "a woman" and then personify "love" as "a murderer." Or mention the word "pedophile" in a song about "drunk girls." My beef is when people talk about how James Murphy has the unique ability to explain my generation to me and I … just don't get it. My pro-This colleagues are right that his lyrics are too hackish to be anything other than meaningless, exactly until the point when somebody tells me they're really about me. And that's exactly the point where I suddenly feel far less charitable and point out that Murphy looks constipated on the cover of his new album. That's retaining your edge.

Which leaves how it sounds. In a technical sense it sounds, like everything Murphy produces, pristine. The best tracks—"Home," "All

I Want," and "I Can Change"—all clearly reference an early '80s palette. This is much cleaner than his early material, as well: "Home" is the only track that really echoes the free-form krautrock palette that was more apparent on his earlier work, and while Murphy still occasionally sticks errant synth lines and percussion riffs into the folds of his tracks, they rarely pull focus. That turns out to be a blessing and a curse—the instrumental portions of This are directionless and sparse in a way that doesn't always complement their length. Combined with the fact that these songs are generally even more straightforward than what he tried on *Sound Of Silver*, the tracks tend to blend together. "Somebody's Calling Me"—a dirge that lasts almost seven minutes, strangling any flow or momentum the album achieves otherwise—is the only true failure here, but the real problem, I think, is that the rest of the album is just so-so. "You Wanted A Hit," "Drunk Girls," "Pow Pow," "Dance Yrself Clean," and "One Touch" all suffer from sounding like other artists, from vamping too long on slight ideas, and from relying on Murphy's personality as much as the musical ideas he commits to them. So, like, the whole Murphy shtick that I just spent paragraphs shitting on is the most distinguishing factor of these tracks, which ends up about as well as you might expect. I've already said "Pow Pow" sounds like Talking Heads, but is it really cool to hear him yell about Barack Obama in his David Byrne voice? And ... what's his point? But "Dance Yrself Clean" is the most egregious example of this problem, and because it starts the album, and because the song itself starts out with the most impressive example of Murphy's self indulgence on This, I can tell you right now: if you've ever had any reason to dislike LCD Soundsystem in the past, it's like he's taunting you.

Actually getting into his music, as it always does, simply requires referencing his touchstone(s) for each song. Which I'm not going to do, because I'm not reviewing other bands. What I will say is the moments of instrumental clarity that emerge from the saccharine sentiments of "Home" remind me why I do believe my above assertion that Murphy is an important figure in music: when he gets a good idea, he knows how to build it into a frenetic rush of sound. But he doesn't really do that anymore, and frankly I wasn't waiting for "You Wanted A Hit," Murphy's ode to the most annoying aspects of the Spoon back catalog. If you hear a vicious dance album that simultaneously captures the ennui of our generation, cool, I guess; we can still go out for a beer. But I just hear a very good producer and very bad writer once again only somewhat succeeding at making a good pop album. Which doesn't make it an atrocity, but neither would referencing Joy Division make it just as good as "Atrocity Exhibition." Just like singing like David Byrne doesn't make you any more capable than Trey Anastasio. Just like referencing David Bowie doesn't make James Murphy anything other than James Murphy. Which isn't a bad thing to be, so what's the big deal?

BALLPARK TUNAGE

David Goldstein
6 April 2010

Rejoice: the 2010 baseball season is upon us. Hope springs eternal, and, as of this writing, both the Toronto Blue Jays and New York Yankees have currently identical win/loss records. Fathers will bring eager sons to the ballpark, 16 ounce Coors Lights will be sold for $7.75, and upon hearing the sounds of the overloud PA systems used in modern ballparks, a vital question will be raised-why do professional baseball players always have such shitty taste in popular music?

This is entirely an assumption based off the many songs I've heard repeatedly played at numerous major league ballparks, it's not like I've actually hung out with the players and quizzed any of them. A major league baseball player is given the liberty of selecting the music that gets played when he comes up to bat or trudges out to the pitcher's mound, and generally speaking, a lamer assortment of tunes you will never find. Standards include Nickelback, Korn, aggro Christian rap-metal mooks POD, and lots of Linkin Park. Man oh man do ballplayers have an unexplained hard-on for Linkin Park. Granted, baseball, even moreso than American football, is not exactly a sport that rewards going against the grain, 'lest you be ostracized from the clubhouse as the dreaded "free spirit." But the music at most ballparks doesn't seem to have evolved beyond 2002, and it's been ages since the game has had a bona fide music nut like '90s hurler "Black" Jack McDowell, a Replacements obsessed starting pitcher who fronted a legitimately decent rock band and used to hang with

Eddie Vedder and REM's Mike Mills.

When Japanese infielder Kazuo Matsui played for the Mets, he came out to bat to the Bruce Lee theme, which was totally cool, and the music guy at late '90s Mets home games used to play Rush's "Limelight" whenever John Olerud strolled to the plate, ostensibly because he's white and Canadian (your move, Jason Bay). I'd be curious to see what wacky San Francisco Giants starter (and reigning NL Cy Young winner) Tim Lincecum rocks out to on his iPod, if only because he looks exactly like Mitch Kramer from Dazed and Confused and therefore totally smokes weed, which was blatantly obvious even before the cops pulled him over and found the stuff in his glove compartment. But these are exceptions to the general rule; I'm more than willing to assume that the majority of ball players still think of Stone Temple Pilots as edgy.

And nowhere is this unoriginality more evident than in the musical selections favored by "closers," the surly relief pitchers entrusted with slamming the door in the ninth inning, securing the final three outs to send everybody home happy. The closest baseball equivalents to the ice hockey goon, ideal closers are supposed to be slightly thuggish, fearless dudes capable of reaching the mid-'90s on their fastball. Their entrance into a game is supposed to strike fear into the hearts of opponents while whipping the home crowd into frenzy, and their introduction music is supposed to reflect this.

So, sigh, this results in plenty of AC/DC, lame Metallica, and modern Reggaeton from those pitchers of a Latin American ilk. Tireless San Diego Padres (now Milwaukee Brewers) closer Trevor Hoffman is often credited with kick-starting the trend, ominously taking the field to the church bell tolling evil of AC/DC's "Hells Bells," which is still somehow novel (when he does it, anyway) after all these years.

"Thunderstruck" and "Welcome to the Jungle" also both get obviously overused in this manner.

Then of course there's Metallica's "Enter Sandman," a groan inducing, stadium-sized pud-pounder that's become so associated with professional sports that you'd be excused for thinking that Major League Baseball commissioned the band to write it. A few years ago when the Mets picked up good 'ol boy Billy Wagner for their ninth inning duties, there was a NY sports media "controversy" because Wagner, and robotic New York Yankees closer Mariano Rivera both used "Enter Sandman" as their introduction music. Wagner was seen as a carpetbagger who "stole" Rivera's song, made even stranger by the fact that Rivera claimed to not actually even like Metallica at all and only listened to "Christian" music. The real controversy here should have been why either of them picked the song at all; true Metallica fans would have realized that entering to "Creeping Death" would have been so much fucking cooler.

If you've read this far, you can guess that yours truly has spent an inordinate amount of time imagining what my "closer music" would be had I skills to accurately throw a baseball harder than 40 miles per hour. Here's a quick list of the three songs that always first come to mind.

The Stooges :: "Down On the Street"

What can possibly be more rock and roll than the first song from the Greatest American Rock Record of All Time? Everything, from Iggy Stooge's inhuman growling, to the whip crack snares evoking gunshots, to the fire breathing wah on Ron Asheton's guitar, reflects the aura of violence and menace that I'd want to evoke if I were going to win one for the home team with a steady diet of 90+ mph fastballs and unhittable breaking stuff. The tune would be especially effective as a hometown rally cry for members of the Detroit Tigers. Detroit fireballer Joel Zumaya is probably going to have to close out a game or two this year. He once openly admitted in 2006 to having to miss playoff games with wrist problems brought on by too much Black Sabbath on Guitar Hero (really). This is his song.

The Pixies :: "Bone Machine"

First the crowd hears the Albini drums, then the Kim Deal bass line, then that immortal D-minor riff and fractured screaming courtesy of Black Francis. In addition to just sounding really cool, while instantly turning any pitcher who used it into an indie-rock pinup, "Bone Machine" would so completely confuse the staid players on the opposing bench that they'd forget to swing the bat. Again, it's highly recommended as a hometown song for Boston Red Sox closer Jonathan Papelbon. But he already uses the Dropkick Murphys' "I'm Shipping Up to Boston," which though perpetuating Boston stereotypes of Irish drunkenness, takes care of the hometown aspect, and is actually a pretty legitimate jam in its own right.

Nirvana :: "Serve the Servants"

Of course, "Smells Like Teen Spirit" is the more obvious choice, and you'd be surprised how very little that song gets played at sporting events (probably because Kurt Cobain is less than family-friendly). But "Serve the Servants" wins out, on account of the ugly-awesome Albini production and the protracted THUD!!! at the start of the song, which again, will totally confuse the crap out of the opposing team.

DEER TICK:
THE BLACK DIRT SESSIONS

Kaylen Hann
26 June 2010

At the end of wrong-doings, carousing, at the end of being hard-done by love, by time, by bros, by ladies, by country, by god and all the above, *The Black Dirt Sessions* (2010) is what's left. Despite being recorded nearly a year ago, this album is the moment John McCauley is finished and the moment he finds in the wake of it all…absolutely fucking nothing. It's the aftermath, and in the aftermath a discovery of a dark, dark personal lack of belief, which proves not only to be substantial but also far emptier than he knew. Or thought he knew: each song a realization of just how empty those black godless hollows are, not only in the world—in the people he knows, the gestures between hands—but also in the blacks residing this whole time just behind his own sternum. The swallowing void that resides so many small, incremental fingers below the clavicle.

Song by song McCauley seems to suss out just how dark it is in his own bones, his own heart, how dark it is behind and just between the ribs, the mouth, the blacks of his belly. Right from the opening "Choir of Angels," where he sings as if he's accompanying his own death, each track begins sounding out those internal spaces. And in turn each song only unearths the shape of what is missing: who's on their way out and what isn't forgiven. Each fragment of his body reveals only more condemnation, unyielding absences, and visceral recesses that just plummet on down and down and down like a bituminous mineshaft into more nothing. His voice taking the brunt force of each fall, acquiring fissures, wrecking itself entirely along the way.

The jangled edges of *War Elephant* (2007) and rascally drive of *Born on Flag Day* (2009), are often replaced by a sullen organ, long bars of bass, strings, piano keys with heavy-ass fingers falling down on them, and intermittent hither-and-thither backups ranging from doo-wop to more traditional folk harmonies: overall favoring melody over fill and gloomy soulfulness over raucousness. Even the brief rock-out moment we're granted in "Mange" is more a sense of damnation realized in some frustrated tangle of a guitar-shredded outro than a moment of indulgence. What makes this (admittedly crawling at times) pace of soulful song after song so tolerable or listenable is— this is some really fucking great writing. From sobered statements like "And the few that care, what have they accomplished right here" to the wrenchingly graphic and curiously tender "Like a heart hung in the sky / A hard-on when I die," it's narrow territory he's covering, but damn is he ever covering it.

Occasionally, in all this solemnity, we catch a brief glint of white off the spine, as he pairs up with the slightest of female vocals for "The Sad Sun," the small lightness of her voice acting as a silver lining or thread-thin stream of brightness to prick through his gathering thunderhead clouds. Or we find ourselves in a sudden warm pulse of heart muscle in the elegiac "Goodbye, Dear Friend."

The clincher, though: "Christ Jesus." The last track of the record, pulled off the debut and like a dead horse beaten back to life—this song just breaks my fucking face. McCauley barks at the darkness, and it barks back. And in this final, infuriating instance he has nothing to say. The extra reverberation around the bass strings as they become less a single note and more a shuddering wire to pull him around by the throat. Piano keys, while usually providing levity of hopeful notes, instead turn to glass and gravel for his voice to belly-crawl across, grating itself down to nothing. Down to fucking nothing. The album ends here, when his voice tires out after pulling its own seams. This last song just leaves him torn up and ground so far into the dirt there's no coming back. There's no song I can really listen to after it—there is no follow-up. I listen to it on loop from there, or I just unplug. Done.

Less about rowdy nights or acknowledging what's coming to him, *The Black Dirt Sessions* is dead-stuck on absolution and the bitter infuriation at this absolution's non-presence: taking stock of what's left in the space at the very end, when he's reached it. And while not punch-for-punch or track-for-track the heavy-hitter *War Elephant* was, or even offering the tonal variety of *Born on Flag Day*, the consistency has come into its own doleful focus, the lyrics have reached a blisteringly high point and for any/all flaws, and, in the end, it just leaves me holding the broken pieces of my face in my fucking hands. And I can't remember the last time the end of an album left me feeling so totally done-for.

CHRISTINA AGUILERA: BIONIC

Lindsay Zoladz
21 June 2010

Christina, you tease us.

And I mean that in a way that truly has nothing to do with the jewel-encrusted ball gag you've been sporting these days. Or the LED heart blinking tastefully over your crotch. Or even the old ass-less chaps hanging in the back of your closet. Really.

What I mean is that you're one of the most high-profile musicians who talks about empowerment in a really fucked-up industry—you write (er, co-write) songs about being a woman who enjoys sex and isn't afraid to express herself, and you sing them in your strato-spherically awesome voice—but then it all kind of falls flat because the sexuality that you're so amped about expressing almost always seems conspicuously similar to whatever particular brand of female sexuality mainstream culture happens to be hocking when your latest album drops. And what's equally frustrating is that you use a pretty myopic kind of pop-feminism as a shield that precludes any criticism of that—you are a singer of songs about being a woman who enjoys sex and isn't afraid to express yourself, thus you can do what you want, thus you don't owe us a damn thing. All of which is totally true. But sometimes I wish you felt like you did owe us something else. Because I, the critic, the lady, and above all things the listener who is continuously disappointed in mainstream pop music and still, naively, continues to put truckloads of faith into it as an awesome and culturally transformative force, am so sick of this shit.

On occasion, Christina Aguilera can do some pretty amazing things, like reduce our knees to jelly with a James Brown tribute or make Chet wax poetic about a performance he admittedly saw on American Idol. She's never quite able to translate that into a solid album though, or even a solid run of a few consecutive singles. So it shouldn't come as a shock that *Bionic* (2010) is not a very good record. What should is that the conversation about how bad it is has become one of the most vitriolic and fascinating conversations pop music has recently provoked.

"I'm not a character," goes the atrociously ironic opening line of the lead-off single, "Not Myself Tonight." The first thing I felt upon seeing the accompanying video—which hit amidst a flurry of half-hearted NSFW!s and a log-in confirmation on Youtube that proved, infallibly, I was over 18—was embarrassment. It's "Bad Romance" without the searing imagery; it seems to ask with hyperactive persistence, "Are you shocked yet? How about now?" Its Gaga and Madonna-aping is as obvious as, well, Gaga's Madonna-aping. But while much of Gaga's appropriation of pop imagery is easy to interpret as homage, the things Christina was quoting were too current to come off as more than a pretty blatant cash-in on Gaga's style. And "Not Myself Tonight" has a pretty dull conception of why people like Lady Gaga so much: glittery bondage gear! bisexuality! Androgyny!—but hey, not too much of that last one, now. In a word, as big as if it were spelled out in the sky by the tailpipe of an airplane: KINK!

The thing that bugged me most about Christina's "homage" to Gaga when I first saw it was that I actually thought it threatened to unravel some of the wonderful things that Gaga's crazy has wreaked on mainstream culture. Say what you will about Gaga: her music, her image, her ugly, and/or her disease—she's done more than any pop star in recent memory to provoke a new conversation about female sexuality and weirdness in pop culture. But by Christina's interpreting "kink" as being narrowly within the limits of Gaga imagery/what mainstream culture has already begun to recognize as kink, it threatens to define the very boundaries of acceptable weirdness. Thankfully, nothing this conceptual actually happened, and all of my overly-academicized handwringing was for naught. The Internet, instead, saw the video and emitted a collective and all-powerful wretch. Christina had stolen from Gaga, the freshly anointed saint of all things pop. People were disgusted. You'd have thought Sinead O'Connor ripped up a picture of the Pope.

So a few weeks later, when the album dropped, anyone who'd seen the video was prepared for Bionic to be an absolute mess. Which it isn't, really. The good thing about Gaga posturing is that it can only be seen and not heard; her music is not distinct enough to be imitable. So though Bionic isn't terribly original, it plunders a pretty wide assortment of things: there's the Right Said Fred-caliber cheese of "Glam," the R. Kelly-isms of "Sex for Breakfast," and the Robyn-esque (though it was co-written by M.I.A.) "Elastic Love," which, stupid as it is, I find faintly enjoyable.

Bionic is, ostensibly, an attempt to re-brand Christina as an electro-pop artist, but its most compelling moments are when it abandons that mission and realizes that that's not the genre in which her voice thrives. "You Lost Me" is an absolute stunner: her voice, minimally adorned, is free to showcase her amazing sense of control and kindle a subtle spectrum of emotion. But, sadly, it's an anomaly. The strings that close the track are barely given a moment to linger before the bombastic, Gary Glitter percussion of "I Hate Boys" smacks the track's quiet subtlety from memory. It's a familiar anthem of what passes for pop-feminist confidence, a song that chants "I hate boys" but spends the rest of the time bragging about how much "boys like me." So by the time you hear the opening query posed by "Vanity"—"Mirror, mirror, on the wall: who's the flyest bitch of them all? Never mind, I am"—you will have completely forgotten that Christina is even capable of subtlety. Or control. Or conceiving that "empowerment" can sometimes mean something more nuanced than tacking on bitch to the end of every other lyric.

So yes, the keeper of one of the best pop voices of our past generation or two is reduced to making shit like this, or is stuck in an industry that insists that she make shit like this. So it goes. But judging from the overwhelming online response—like, not just from stodgy critics who treat Gaga like she's Judith Butler in a wig (raising my hand), but from everybody—to Christina's new "character," I'm compelled to read a little bit of naive hope into this post-Gaga, post-Internet moment in pop music: maybe people are finally a little more willing to see through the boring, faux-transgressive schlock that mainstream culture feeds us; maybe people are ready to demand something else. And maybe the Internet better enables people to express that. (Or maybe, less hopefully, more likely: people just enjoy Lady Gaga's music, and the Internet enables them to pounce upon Christina with the same lynch-mob mentality with which they dismiss every pop star who suddenly seems irrelevant. Whatever.) What Christina has over Gaga—minus the obvious voice thing—is that she doesn't have to pander to her listeners with safe, middling electro-pop just to stay embedded in mainstream culture. She's already there. So the door remains open for her to finally do something daring and awesome. And we, or I, at least, will foolishly cling to the hope that someday she might take up that challenge.

STARFLYER 59:
THE CHANGING OF THE GUARD

Chris Molnar
23 September 2010

In his review for 2008's *Dial M*, Conrad asserted that "the best move
this band can make isn't stylistic but personal." In other words, the
negative effects of Christianity make Starflyer 59's persistence within
the Christian music industry immoral and inconsistent with their
large, quality, and rarely religious body of work. I disagree: for me,
as with Conrad, it was the impressive original roster of Tooth & Nail
which helped make the bizarre nature of a Christian upbringing
bearable. Those bands, including the Danielson Famile, Poor Old
Lu, and eventually MewithoutYou, remain common points between
me and anyone from a similar background. If I hadn't heard Pedro
the Lion's *Whole EP* (1997)—released on Tooth & Nail—in the
listening booth at Family Christian Stores, it would've taken me that
much longer to emerge from the bubble, to grapple with the imma-
teriality of the limits Christian music imposes on itself. Labels like
Tooth & Nail seemed to once grapple in secret, hiding bands more
ambiguously identified with Christian music behind a brand permis-
sible to religious parents while introducing variety and perspective
to music-hungry teenagers allowed precious little. They are, in other
words, doing God's work.

So where does all this leave Starflyer and *The Changing Of The
Guard* (2010)? In many ways, Jason Martin's ongoing project chases
trends in the same way that Christian rock is often derided for doing

so—it's just that he does it as well or better than many of his secular peers, and with a distinctive flair. *Silver* (1994), *Gold* (1995), and *Americana* (1997) were often impenetrable responses to My Bloody Valentine and the shoegaze movement, heavy albums (with monochrome covers that echoed their walls of guitar) that belied a sly pop sense. When Martin changed altogether for *The Fashion Focus* (1998), sacrificing heaviness for lush, sweet-spot arrangements, his defiant melancholy emerged as if out of nowhere, buoyed instead of buried by Pumpkins-era riffage. Ever since *Focus* and its immediate successors, *Everybody Makes Mistakes* (1999) and *Leave Here A Stranger* (2001), his productions have grown more assured, if never as transcendent, developing into sophisticated, dark, welcome slices of indie rock. There is a mix of aggression and maturity on songs like "I Win," a synth-hook dance number from 2006's *My Island*, or the squealing power pop of "New Wife, New Life" from 2003's *Old*, that infuse the grownup blues of bands like The National or The Walkmen with a youthful tension. Borne perhaps out of slogging for two decades through an industry that would probably be happier without him, one he could probably make far more money outside of, it's the sound of a man who isn't just conflicted about his place in society, but conflicted about the fundamental ideas that underlie his musical existence.

In that way, Starflyer is everything the Christian music industry could and ought to be, and *The Changing Of The Guard* is no different: the first and best song, "Fun is Fun," is yet another in a long line of Starflyer songs that combines unexpected influences with Jason Martin's thick burden of doubt, leavened by a knack for unlimited hooks. There's some Panda Bear gamelan in the intro, an impeccable George Harrison-style slide guitar in the chorus; these are inscrutably brought together by the masterfully delivered line "Fun is fun / And done is done." Martin's deep, halting, yet ultimately warm baritone is reminiscent now of Matt Berninger while both predating it and outgunning it in depth; the authoritative, half-smiling reprimand could apply equally to sinners, to Christian music, to himself. And still it could mean anything, or nothing, content to exist simply as the catchiest part of a near-perfect pop song.

Starflyer's koans manage to turn the theological angst of someone like Sufjan Stevens into brooding, populist anthems as opposed to book-ish niche fodder. "I was born a trucker's son" goes "Trucker's Son," and while the perfunctory lead guitar might not elevate it into the pantheon of great Starflyer songs, the hard simplicity of the lyrics—Martin really is a trucker's son, supporting himself throughout his career by driving for his father's company—inspires questions of class and inheritance that peers like David Bazan or Daniel Smith pose far more concretely … and awkwardly. If anything, the fault of Guard is that finally, maybe, the intelligent dissatisfaction that has produced Martin's best work is becoming old hat. Songs like "Coconut Trees" race through the kinds of guitar leads and layering that used to be luxurious and patient on such aching, misty pop as *Mistakes*'s "Play The C Chord" or *Fashion Focus*'s heartbroken, heartbreaking "Fell In Love At 22," possibly the apex of his career.

Maybe the balance Martin achieved between Christian insularity, post-adolescent nostalgia, and a wised-up sense of irony has finally started to fail him as he enters middle age. I'm not too concerned, though, as long as he can still whip curveballs like the baroque "Kick the Can," all no-nonsense guitar and smooth vocals. Even those who disagree with his loyalty to a label associated with the church—and which has long since given up having more than a few decent bands at a time—would be hard pressed to deny that he represents everything that could be and is good about any genre dedicated to an ideology.

Able to work the opposite track of an unabashed proselytizer like Brother Danielson, introducing grown-up doubts to Christians instead of child-like faith to atheists, Martin's one of the best craftsmen in pop, in any industry, still giving Christian teens a glimpse of ambiguously non-secular, forward-thinking music—personally valuable, to me at least. "It haunts me in my sleep / And comes back when I'm awake / I think I'm gonna lose my mind," he says in the closing song. "I've got a bad feeling in my bones / Could it be because I went it alone?" he asks, and that, depending on how one comes across Starflyer 59, this could suggest a failure to rely on God, a failure to rely on bandmates (he is the only consistent member of the band), or the end of a romance—or all three—is one of the pleasures in witnessing an artist haunt the rears of a haunted industry.

SUFJAN STEVENS: THE AGE OF ADZ

Dom Sinacola
23 October 2010

No argument: *The Age of Adz* (2010) is the work of a terribly talented guy. Shit is bristling with talent, voluptuous with it—but also beholden to it? See, no one's arguing Sufjan Stevens isn't a singular artist; no one's trying to rain on his parade or tell him what's what; no one's hoping he'll stop being such an ambitious cultural Katamari ball, leveling genre distinctions as if they're pleasant picket fences dividing identical shades of green. No one's even really that peeved that his albums are always concept albums even when they aren't. Everything he does is big and labored and exhaustive, which just means that everything he's done has always had the potential to be exhausting. And no one is criticizing Stevens' ace in the hole: his innate comprehension of arrangements, and the way that, animal, vegetable, or mineral, he is able to rein all of his sound into a fastidiously embroidered corset that binds and holds in his swollen, melancholy core. And since we all know what Sufjan Stevens' sad, sad heart sounds like, maybe *The Age of Adz* is just that same, beautiful sound, only now in technicolor. Because obviously this is his best record, right? Because it's just a lot more of everything we already liked?

I think we're overlooking some crucial information here. Perhaps the glow of Stevens' ego is blinding our ultra-sensitive eyeballs. I'm not sure if the way *The Age of Adz* has been received, heralded, and kept bereft of salient criticism is due to the relatively long length of time between it and *Illinois* (2005), or due to how universally accepted Stevens' existential and emotional crises have been, or even due to the simple realization that we're no longer buying a Sufjan Stevens album but instead Stevens himself. What I am sure of is that *The Age of Adz*, bastion of ambition and aspiration in the face of your typical uninterested indie posture or not, isn't all that special. It's the big box store of Sufjan Stevens albums: something for everyone, but it's easy to get lost in the wrong aisle.

See, it's not that Calum's totally wrong with the basic details: after five years of waiting to see what Stevens would do next, we're finally offered a Stevens who's subverted his intentions with the States Project to inflate his own narrative, "making his personal history sound like the history of the world." Sure, but…have we all forgotten about *Seven Swans* (2004)? On the heels of *Michigan* (2003) and as a quiet precursor to the majesty of *Illinois*, Swans was clear evidence that Stevens had, at the core of all his bombast, a singer-songwriter heart with a penchant for extremely touching melody. The title track of that album, especially, presents a microcosm of what we've grown to know intrinsically, over the past decade, about Stevens' craft: the song is long, it aches with spiritual struggle, it grows towards a climax meant to stir goosebumps from subcutaneous slumber, it exposes his atavistic dread and guilt, and it chides us into accepting his struggle as a universal constant. "Seven Swans" is, for these reasons, an appallingly gorgeous song, and also—despite its seven minutes and choir of voices and grand narratives delivering in gasping, sacred detail a Fatima-like portent blazing in the sky—a concise piece of epic folk. Every instrument has a place, a purpose, and together the purposes collude; when they fuse I'm ravished.

Similar synergy seems like it's going to happen throughout *The Age of*

Adz. The title track rages out of the gate with fireworks fizzles and spaceship landing noises and strings trilling their brains out—hell, Stevens seeming utterly spent in under 50 seconds. But "Adz" only mounts in calamity from there. The title "Too Much" is just a cute joke; the song suggests there are apparently never too many rhythmic components to run through "mermaid farting" filters. " I Walked" maps the same landscape, as does "Now That I'm Older" after it, as does "Get Real Get Right," and so on until the already much-bally-hooed "Impossible Soul" crams 25 minutes down our already exhausted brainpans, getting away with Auto-tune, cheerleading, whatever else is left of any modern mainstream detritus to which Stevens has been partial in the past five years. Even "Bad Communi-cation," the album's shortest track at all of two and a half minutes, throbs impatiently with lazer zaps, bloops, blibbles, splashes of turpentine, more and more voices, kadiddles, a mandolin maybe, the ploopy facsimile of E.T. picking his nose—I am running out of conceivable onomatopoeia for this crap.

I'm sure you get the point. And by "you," I mean one of two kinds of people on this planet: those who see *The Age of Adz* as half full, and those who see it as half empty. Or, to use Stevens' vernacular: those who see the album as too much and…those who see the album as too much. Because I think we all see the same thing here (and him scaling the Billboard charts means he's reaching more "you"s than ever)—we all see an album absolutely aureate. We all see something loaded to the gills, pulsing with ambition.

Please don't get me wrong: I'm not trying to draw a line in the sand here, to encourage our readers to pick a side, mine or Calum's, and then from my Hate Fort whip mudballs at Calum's cherubic face lit rosy by the enjoyment of *The Age of Adz*, his attention ignorant of my grumblings because he's focused on the limitless heavens while

I'm steaming in the gutter. See, I think it's pretty obvious that Calum and I are talking about the same thing here. He calls him Sufjan and I call him Stevens; he's a big fan who's been waiting for this for a long time, interest only mildly piqued by the *All Delighted People* EP (2010), and so am I, scout's honor; he sees *The Age of Adz* as the latest testament to ambition from an insanely prolific musician, and so do I. But where Calum revels in that glut, loving how Suf's peeled back the distance of his historic narratives while re-peeling the stinky onion of his globular sound, I find a musician at his most unsure, no longer in control of his mighty talent and ambition, no longer capable, as he was on "Seven Swans"—as he was on *Michigan* and *Illinois*—of making essential music.

Consider: "I'm not fucking around," Stevens declares, working blue, knowing he's never used such language in public before, but by that point, waist-deep in the cosmic mess of "I Want To Be Well," we already know that. *The Age of Adz* is not the sound of a guy fucking around; in fact, it's far from anything I'd call "fun." It is long, harrowing, sometimes even thankless, like long division with too many remainders or an unbalanced equation with Xs, Ys, and Zs hanging in the ethereal void to forever remain unfilled. It's math; it's empirically, logically unempirical. It is indescribably overblown. And voila: people fall all over themselves to unlock the secret of this new, experimental approach Stevens is taking to music, conveniently forgetting that he ended *Illinois* with a near-perfect homage to Steve Reich's Music for 18 Musicians that also worked thematically in the context that album. All of this particular clatter doesn't add up to much beyond a claustrophobic awareness of the UI grids that mark off measures in whatever DAW Stevens stitched this stuff together. Because let's be clear: *The Age of Adz* is unsettling not because Stevens deploys this new palette; it's unsettling because he's had five years to figure out how to make this shit work and…it really doesn't, I don't think. The new experience this album provides, at least to me, is that for the first time you can hear the seams of Stevens' overwhelming arrangements.

And even that would be fine, since the other thing that nobody is arguing is that Stevens must necessarily remain tied to an acoustic, intimate, confessional aesthetic, or that overdubbing wasn't a necessary component of his previous works. The problem I have is that this sound that Calum sees as exciting and rife with possibility I find unnerving: "when will 'Vesuvius' fall apart?", I wonder. "Is it when its sweet and awe-struck melody is overrun by that obnoxious squeal Stevens shunts into the midst of an otherwise hushed, patient piano ballad? Not to mention the background gibbering, the gasket-blowing 'beat,' the endless echoes, the flute-lead intermission shat all over by that infernal squeal?" I can just imagine that conversation in the studio: "OK, I'm going to give you a kazoo and a distortion pedal, and on the thirtieth time I sing the refrain I want you to just flat-out ruin the whole song. Sorry: fucking song." It's infuriating to listen to Stevens kill every pretty, unadorned idea, and then beat every tainted idea to fucking death. And that's when the excitement of this album becomes a chore, when a song's already tumbled in on itself and the listener can either give up or strain through the rabble to find the one sound, the one note or splash of humility, to keep the thing grounded. And even that approach is flawed, frankly. Consider the middle section of "Impossible Soul," the album's triumphant, cheerleading-led, anthemic centrepiece, so exhilarating for the four minutes or so that it lasts. Some might find solace there, but in the midst of a 25-minute track, bookended by auto-tuned vocals and portentous builds and ebbs, this beautiful moment is so underlined and highlighted and starred and bookmarked as the clear thematic Moment of Clarity for the rest of the album that it becomes its own negation. And then, to make sure that point is driven home, the entire sequence is essentially replayed at half-speed, which...valid creative decision? Sure. Fun to listen to? Meh.

It's perplexing. Stevens seemingly knows enough about complex song structures and composition that it seems odd that he's built each of these songs and then layered such incongruous, distracting, un-earned, manic noise on top of them—which is another frustrating issue, because rarely does the noise seem integrated into the song structures. He's done the intimacy thing before; he's pared down his talent before; all this he's done before, but never before has his work been so buffeted on all sides by contradictions: that glut is the same as ambition; that ambition is enough because it's ambitious; that spare, colloquial lyrics are concise; that electronic instruments only make electronic music; that *A Sun Came* (2000) and *Know Your Rabbit* (2001) represent both past Stevens and future Stevens; that Sufjan Stevens is alone in his existential crises, his problems volumi-nous enough to sink this noisy world. CMG's Mark Abraham has pointed out that the closest analogy to *The Age of Adz* he can think of is Todd Rundgren's *A Wizard, A True Star* (1973), another tortured, labored example of a studio genius drowning his own work in half-assed gropes towards "experimentation" but still offering, in the form of "Just One Victory," a stunning example of cathartic release. It's a sad comparison, because that album essentially marked the end of Rundgren's relevance as a musician and composer in his own right.

Here's hoping that doesn't happen to Stevens. See, I used to get inspired by him, and I still want to be: here is someone who has talent on a level I can only dream of; here is someone who comes from the same area where I come from; who writes about all the places that influenced me deeply throughout my whole life; and who, despite his grandiosity, speaks with such warm understanding of all the homes and people who have shaped me as a music fan and as an aspiring artist. But I can't not be confused that *The Age of Adz* is as shameless is as it is. I don't want to say Calum's wrong, because I can't experience his experience with this album. But when Calum talks about how the lyrics are so personal and first person, that Stevens is no longer playing characters, I have to admit that the music itself, at least to me, belies that notion: where he used be be so proficient at letting us hear the sound of his sad, sad heart, the directionless elliptical clutter that defines *The Age of Adz* just sounds to me like he's manufacturing an idea of what a sad heart might sound like. What's worse, it sounds self-indulgent.

But maybe we should have expected this? Really, the criticisms I'm levying at *The Age of Adz* are not so different than the criticisms I defended *Illinois* against in 2005. That was, for some, a bloated album. The difference, I think, amounts to two things: the bloat with *Illinois* was the album's length (and the ludicrous song titles). But more importantly, Illinois could be grandiose because it was part of such a grandiose—and, in hindsight, possibly self-defeating—project. But we adapted. Before *The Age of Adz*, those of us who had carried a candle for Stevens had, as the years since Illinois grew and the death of the 50 States project became apparent, decided that we would be just as happy with something simpler: something that didn't aspire to encapsulate a whole region, something without lengthy song-titles, something that doesn't have to answer to a whole state's population, but only Sufjan himself. It turns out that was not so impossible; it turns out this is exactly what *The Age of Adz* is.

Boy, we made such a mess together.

INTERLUDE: FAKE DAN BEJAR LYRICS

Staff

"The wine of their eyes tasted like juniper / Oh god, Jupiter / you are a big planet."

"The dresser is on fire, but not the best to know aflame'd / Chicago is two, great! / My loins, in first."

"She wrapped her halo 'round her ear lobe / falling on the fickle fjords of fashion. / Not as innocent as those blue jeans / so bourgeois blues on me. / O' Diana—the moon is made of CURDS NOT CHEESE!"

"'A coterie aloof!' / called the lamb to its hoof / and the garland of the dook was not overtly preoccu-pieduh."

"On able ankles, 'absolutely!'—but truly we're fixating on fiction. / Ungainly looms the bitten groom; his diction is surface-deep."

"Oh: Homunculus. / Your ho-hum homonyms—oh, monk, you lust. / You name our humble human murmurs a numbered calculus. / Oh: homunculus."

"Desire is a threaded weasel / baring teeth at passing women. / I once thought / there was no finer trapper of weasels / than you. / But then I discovered / that Scott Weiland's solo album / is only $14.99 on

Amazon.com. / His lyrics are quite brilliant. / Nosferatu!"

"Zounds! / Mirthless anecdotes abound!/ Persnickety and trite, / she was wilting in the tiger's eye. / Once capricious and profound: ALIVE!"

"'Destroy!' / she yelled atop her griffin, bespeckled in dusted velour. / She was a barista with hopes of venom—chocolate dust and cinnamom twists injustices. / A businessman with a cellphone earpiece mouthed, 'Cobra! Cobra! Cobra!' in her ear. / This song is about World War 2."

"Gene's hubris is larval. / The stewardess too rapacious / to marvel at how many drinks he's ordered. / Scrimshaw skies and Inuit glyphs. / The cumulus like eyelets / and nimbus a cold iris."

MIRACLE FORTRESS: WAS I THE WAVE?

Jessica Faulds
24 May 2011

Moving to Quebec (and Montreal in particular) from elsewhere in Canada is something of a mindfuck. Not only is there a flip in official languages—so that an inability to scrape "r"s across your palate marks you as an outsider, and regional dialects change block by block—but there is history: actual textbook, dead-white-guy stuff that makes it seem like everything important in post-colonization Canada from Jacques Cartier to Pierre Trudeau to the Arcade Fire came from right here, this bagel-studded hub on the St. Lawrence River.

In the last decade or so, Montreal's sense of cultural importance has only grown, largely due to what's happening here musically. The most important bands the city has produced are not just big, but iconic (think Leonard Cohen, Godspeed! You Black Emperor, and, of course, the Arcade Fire), and the gaps between them are filled with a pretty respectable group of standbys (Wolf Parade, Chromeo, Kid Koala) and up-and-comers (Braids, Grimes, Little Scream), all of which set the bar pretty high for other municipalities vying for the title of Cultural Capital. From outside, it is easy to imagine these groups are all in it together somehow, floating in an incredible primordial soup of creativity, and occasionally popping their heads up in various configurations to release albums. This theory of interconnectedness is probably what led me to go see any band touring to my hometown with the words "from Montreal" scrawled beneath their name on a poster, however shittily Xeroxed. However, since I moved to the city itself, what I've seen is that it's not so different from other places: pockets of musicians working together and alone to create music of varying quality.

It is from this older and wiser perspective that I now re-approach Miracle Fortress, one of the Montreal artists floating in the gel of acclaim that lubes this city's every musical offering, and creator of my favorite album of 2007, *Five Roses*. When that record dropped, it was swiftly vaulted into the annals of Canadian critical success and nominated for the Polaris Prize, but outside of that friendly national bubble, several reviewers accused it of ripping off Brian Wilson (in 2007, the official year of ripping off Brian Wilson!) and "failing to inspire awe." Never mind that it had beautiful melodies for miles and an overall luminescent shimmer like a glitter-spackled swimming pool—it just wasn't awe-inspiring. Of course, if being original and striking critics dumb with a sense of the sublime were requirements for critical acclaim, Best Coast wouldn't have had such a banner year in 2010. So, perhaps part of the reason some were so tight-fisted with their praise of *Five Roses* was really that from Montreal bands, we do sometimes expect spectacle, expect boundary-nudging, expect awe. I mean, hello Colin Stetson!

So, for those looking for an epiphanic listening experience, I should probably mention right here that Miracle Fortress has once again failed to, like, shift the zeitgeist. *Was I The Wave?* (2011)is, like its predecessor, a solid, carefully thought out collection of songs that trades in nubbly textures and stealth vocal lines that hook into co-chlea and don't let go. In fact, that may be one of the only ways *Was I The Wave?* resembles *Five Roses*. The two releases will probably be classified in the same genre only because "indie rock" means pretty much everything. *Was I The Wave?* shows Graham Van Pelt (the man behind the fortress) following in step with the rest of us, transferring a penchant for 'verbed out guitars to a lust for undulating synths and drum samples, and landing at a kind of anaesthetized dance pop. Something of *Five Roses'* shimmer remains, yet here it serves as a green screen backing Van Pelt's synth tinkering, robotic drums, and runs up to falsetto. The resulting "bedroom club," as Van Pelt has dubbed it, is a little dreamy, but also little seductive. You know, recommended if you like: sleep sex.

There's a little strangeness here, too. Van Pelt isn't afraid of instrumental tracks, which allow him to flex his studio muscles, stewing and stretching various sounds, holding them up in various states of melt. He also doesn't resist the urge to take what might be a three-minute pop song and derail it, as in "Tracers," which seems to be a straight up 808-inspired dance nugget until it drops all melody and veers into a straight 75 seconds of (I'm going to use some technical jargon here) doop-a-doop-a-doops. The series of bippy notes starts sparse but are soon layered, and as they multiply over the unceasing drum machine, internal melodies emerge, not quite tonal, but contoured, like chains of bubbles popping, like ordered patterns of mold surfacing in petri dish culture. It's, well, kind of weird. So while Van Pelt's music couldn't accurately called experimental, he still has his moments of smearing his fingers around in paint.

And no matter which tropes he's working with, Van Pelt can always rely on his melodic sense to keep them from feeling played out. He doesn't have the earth-shattering vocal abilities of some of his compatriots, but his melodies are undeniable—catchy, but subtle enough that when he kicks the intensity up a notch, it is more affecting than a cavalcade of carefully orchestrated harmonies. I mean, when Fleet Foxes sing, the sky opens up and the heavens ring, and blah, blah,

blah, but in "Spectre," as he articulates how it feels to be losing a game of catch-up and sings, "Try to feel the way we felt much younger," Van Pelt reaches a higher plane without even raising his voice.

Miracle Fortress has never been at the forefront of trends. Graham Van Pelt sits a few seats back taking it all in, and makes his appearance just before the curtain closes on a particular fad. He was the sun-kissed '60s just when indie was getting sick of pretty, and now he's apparently in on the '80s-nostalgic dance pop, just when the slacker '90s seem to be making their comeback. And so, in answer to this album's titular question: no. With all due respect, Miracle Fortress was not the wave, at least where "the wave" is a metaphor for the thrust that pushes the world forward. Van Pelt is not designing sounds to blow us into a new paradigm, but crafting textures to drawn us in, to subsume, to mesmerize, and perhaps, through a combination of these effects, to softly awe. The album's cover is probably a better indicator than its title of what can be heard between the grooves of this record. Though Van Pelt is not the wave, he may be the endless blue.

I DID NOT HAVE FUN: LOLLAPALOOZA 2011

Colin McGowan
19 August 2011

Deadmau5 was doing whatever Deadmau5 does. I had stopped looking at the stage and was instead fixated on a blotch of mustard that had fallen on my shoe. I licked my thumb and squatted over my feet to wipe the stain. Nestled in a forest of tan leg fat, I saw a small hand with bright red fingernails making a circular motion some four inches below the hem of a teenage girl's skirt. I saw the hand glide up the girl's skirt like a spider caught in an updraft and fumble for a moment as if it were turning a combination lock. I was in middle school once; I know that clumsy motion. There was some serious fingering going on while Deadmau5 was doing whatever Deadmau5 does.

This was the low point of the weekend. Also that weekend I saw the Cool Kids, the Mountain Goats, and a sampling of other bands. By "sampling," I mean I spent most of my time ping-ponging between stages, flipping through the Lolla app on my phone, trying to link sounds I didn't like with band names I had heard of once or twice, avoiding stuff I was positive I would hate. Did *Gorilla vs. Bear* tepidly approve of those guys' first record? Well, they're probably better than Soundgarden. I may have seen Local Natives, who I remember sorta hating at last year's Pitchfork Music Festival. I saw some band that played boring folk pop. Fuck whatever band that was.

I went to Lollapalooza alone. That's not true, technically, but I was alone at Lollapalooza. In part because AT&T's network was apparently manned by carrier pigeons the entire weekend; texts arrived 45 minutes after they were sent, which made meeting up impossible. Some people I know wanted to see Skrillex, and I wanted to grab some free booze from the press tent rather than pay $5 for a Bud Light. We parted ways, and with no trail of electronic breadcrumbs to lead us back to each other, never reunited.

Which is fine. I sorta hate Skrillex the way I sorta hate that band I'm pretty sure was Local Natives. It's a microwaveable sort of hate, because unlike my id or the Chicago Transit Authority, I get to choose how much contact I have with Skrillex or Local Natives or Ratatat. I'm not the guy to make faces at other people having fun.

Or: I am, but I don't want to be that guy, as I am also the guy who has friends and acquaintances and acquaintances' cousins who were looking forward to this weekend in roughly the same measure I was dreading it. In fact, two friends from New York drove cross-country to sleep on my floor and see Eminem. I think all of these people have bad taste in music, and they probably think I'm an asshole. We try not to vocalize these sentiments to each other.

Lollapalooza is a festival for people who believe in festivals, people whose hands get all clammy for, like, the Drums and who think a weekend of music can be transformative. It's also a festival for thirtysomethings who want to get fucked up, lay in the sun, and pretend they're twenty again. It's a festival for people who want to do mushrooms and look at pretty colors—but then, that's every music festival, and the euphoria of tripping has a lot more to do with the fireworks going off in one's head than any specific corporeal thing. Anyhow, Chicago is a city with enough pretty colors that don't form a Playstation logo to avoid a festival like this and still have a fine time hallucinating.

Lollapalooza is not a festival for me, who, without a node to cling to in this sea of (I guess) pretty happy people, can only cling to pettiness. I thought about writing that Skrillex's set sounded like an asshole tumultuously shitting out teeth without having seen his set, but that felt unfair. Not because I don't have valid criticisms to lob at Skrillex or the glitter-pocked sewage monster that is Lollapalooza, but because the sewage monster has its slimy paws wrapped around a mass of humans—douchebags, teens, parents, lawyers, the drunk, the severely depressed, the mourning, the people who like me ate some rancid hotdogs and had to throw up only moments before leaving for the festival, the Chris Cornell fans, whatever—who seem (I guess) pretty happy. I let ice cream trucks roll by my apartment all the time without lecturing the local 8-year-olds about maintaining a healthy diet. And it's not like I don't eat ice cream.

The most gracious thing I can offer Lollapalooza is a mutual understanding that we should stay the hell away from each other. Let chain-smoking Dads pump their fists. Let the muddy masses undulate to shitty electronica. Let Anheuser-Busch plaster its logo onto the blood platelets of infants. Let Deadmau5 do whatever Deadmau5 does. Let the children finger-fuck. I just don't want to watch it.

DISMEMBERMENT PLAN

Lindsay Zoladz
26 January 2011

The only thing better than a great memory is waking up the next morning to the thought that you will get to live it all over again. Such was the liminal state of reverie in which I walked around my neighborhood all Saturday afternoon, poised between the Dismemberment Plan's two back-to-back reunion shows in their fiercely yet endearingly possessive hometown of Washington, D.C. There was a single moment during Friday's set at the Black Cat, which will maybe go down as one of my personal favorite moments at the venue, when the city's mounting fervor over the band's homecoming seemed to reach a fever pitch. Travis Morrison stood alone on stage beside a small Yamaha keyboard, manning the endearingly chintzy beat of "You Are Invited," and behind him the rest of the band began to filter back out onto the stage: Eric Axelson strapped on his mighty bass; Jason Caddell slung his guitar over his shoulder; Joe Easley, head dwarfed by his ubiquitous air traffic controller headphones, sat down behind his kit. By the time Morrison got to the part in the song where he talks to his ex in the kitchen, the air was taut with what we all knew was about to come. A few people scattered around the crowd wearing birthday hats held cans of Silly String aloft. Strangers grinned at each other with that conspiratorial look right before the guest of honor walks into a surprise party. I don't know that I've ever seen a place so ready to blow.

But before that Silly String goes flying, let's set the ol' memory machine back at least a couple of days, to a time when most D.C. residents within a two-decade age span were clamoring with anticipation and nostalgia over the band's imminent return. Nearly every local publication ran a series of articles about the band and their legacy, scene veterans eagerly tried to one-up each other's I Was There stories, and the recently reissued *Emergency & I* (1999) seemed to be playing inside every pair of headphones in the city. I had not seen critics and laypeople united in such a collective tizzy over music since, well, y'know.

Even in their absence (they broke up in 2003 but played a pair of D.C. shows in 2007), the D-Plan have maintained an emotional stranglehold over many of their fans; otherwise stoic grown-ups are given to telling their "I got on stage for 'Ice Of Boston'" stories in the same tone of voice they reserve for stories about losing their virginities. It makes sense: the band was in the business of unabashedly mining the dormant emotions of early adulthood. Through Morrison's lyrics and the mechanized warmth of their music, they laid bare the secret truths of fledgling adulthood and urban malaise that everybody more or less feels but often acts too together, or too old, to say aloud: that a life of endless possibilities is often more crippling than it is freeing, that opening your heart to other people is sometimes the hardest fucking thing in the world, and that the everyday mechanical grind of city life is crushing, heartwarming, alienating, lonely, poetic, and often times all of these things at once.

But any Washingtonian will tell you that there's something about the Plan's perspective that's particular to D.C. Of course, there's the city's music history, and the way they fit into a local narrative of innovative punk: their reign as Best Band In Town spanned the couple of years between Fugazi and Q and Not U. But their connection to the rhythms of this city runs a little deeper than even the surrounding musical landscape. I didn't get it when I first moved here, and I certainly didn't get it the first time I heard *Change* (2001) or *Emergency & I*, but now entering my sixth year living here, I think I do. There's something about this city that's particularly disillusioning and prone to the sort of slap-happy eyeball rolls you can almost hear an audible echo of in Travis Morrison's voice: it's what you feel as a not-that-young-anymore-and-not-entirely-together person living in a city that stands as a metonym for a polished, successful and stately idea of adulthood to which you're pretty sure you will never live up. It's in the feeling of riding the Metro during the Federal employees' rush hour, your sneakers beside their expensive briefcases as you sit in a t-shirt that bespeaks the alliterative name of the restaurant or cupcake shop where you work. It's the feeling of going downtown to collect an unemployment check in a building that's within the line of sight of the White House or the Supreme Court or the Washington Monument—a skyline of empty, dignified stone that seems to leer at you when you can't live up to its unattainable standard of success. That particular strand of disillusionment and the life that kicks so fiercely beneath it is what the Dismemberment Plan were able to articulate more precisely than any band before or since. Just listen to the first minute of "Spider In The Snow": the way the chilly synth washes over the ever-forward gait of Axelson's bass line and the deadpan intonation of Morisson's "I would walk down K Street to some temping job / As winter froze the life out of fall / Yeah, I must have been having a ball" say more about trying to cobble together a life in Washington than any monument ever will.

So that's what was behind the conspiratorial look we were all sharing when the band pounded into the second chorus of "You Are Invited" and the Silly String went flying into the rafters. The Black Cat show was the first and the smallest of the three shows the band would play in D.C that weekend, and being in a tight space gave their frenetic, two-hour set the benefit of intimacy. From the unexpected opener "Soon To Be Ex-Quaker," it was a set surprisingly heavy on the spazzy stuff (the chaotic singalong "Dismemberment Plan Gets Rich" being an undeniable highlight in that category), but there was plenty of room for some much beloved slowburners too ("Ellen And Ben," "Rusty," "Superpowers"). Pretty much everyone I talked to that night left in a state of awe at how a band that hadn't played together in almost a decade could sound so tight.

Saturday's performance at the 9:30 Club proved the old show-going adage that the bigger the venue, the more likely you will be able to discern what the people around you were drinking by smelling your clothes the next morning. I always seem to have a similar experience at this club, and this time was no exception, as even in the second row (you know, up there with the people who supposedly really like music) I ended up standing in front of two girls who chattered through all the slow songs, sloshed poorly-gripped gin and tonics into my hair, and between songs saw fit to yell the rather cumbersome "TRAVISUNBUTTON ANOTHER BUTTON ON YOUR SHIRT," much to the embarrassment of everyone else standing in the section of the crowd from which that comment reached the stage. (I don't even want to tell you what was coming out of their mouths during "Girl O'Clock.") But as always, this experience is an almost-worthwhile trade-off for the 9:30 Club's commanding soundsystem, which made the band sound positively soaring during the chorus of "What Do You Want Me To Say," and which maximized the gutpunch when that yowl of a guitar line cuts through Easley and Axelson's kinetic percussion on "The Other Side." As always, the guys also found an opportunity to affirm their love of pop music: closing number "OK, Joke's Over" had embedded within its extended bridge an inspired cover of Far East Movement's "Like A G6"—a fitting statement, since, as you can imagine from where I was standing Morrison by that point had the sober girls acting drunk and the drunk girls acting real drunk.

The chance to experience this sort of thing two nights in a row allows for one to perform controlled experiments in show-going: one night drunk and one night sober; one night with friends and one night alone; one night watching "The Ice Of Boston" from the crowd and one night living out the dream of screaming, "OH FINE MOM, HOW'S WASHINGTON?" with about a hundred other ecstatic people on stage. For when the dozens of shaky, front row iPhone videos finally emerge: that's me in the yellow skirt, jumping up and down next to Morrison for the first five seconds of the song, and then, in a deluge of dudes, promptly getting pushed back to the furthest corners of the stage and into a line of sight where I could not see the crowd or the flashbulbs in front of me but from which I was able to gather for you this bit of reportage: Joe Easley plays the drums better than you do in your dreams, and guess what, he does it barefoot.

The overwhelming sense of community at these shows was particularly and belatedly gratifying to me, since my own personal D-Plan narrative is more of an I Wasn't There story. I picked up a copy of *!* (1995) on a whim at a used record store only a couple of years ago. When I got the album home and looked at the track list, I was startled to find a song called "13th & Euclid"—I'd just moved into a basement apartment on that very corner only about a week before. The Plan's approach to punk immediately reminded me of the Minutemen's approach to punk: not as a dictum on how to sound or what sort of haircut to sport, but as an entire ideology of creative freedom—a blank slate for a defiantly personal perspective. Still, "13th & Euclid" stood as a metaphor for the way I felt about my connection the band—and in a lot of ways, that spectral ideology of

D.C. punk—it was almost maddening to know that all of that had happened right here, but that a decade later those memories seemed to be the possessions of time, not space.

So, unlike most of the people who were living here in the band's heyday, my love of the Plan's music has felt singular and isolated. Last year this feeling became even more pronounced, when I was coping with a close friend's death and *Change* was quite literally the only record that existed for me in those first couple of weeks. Having the chance to finally be in an entire roomful of people singing the lyrics to "The Other Side" or "Following Through" was not just an exercise in personal catharsis, but it felt like a strange moment of past collapsing into present—the making of a common memory.

Even if ?uestlove can't make the Dismemberment Plan reunite for longer than the couple of shows they have scheduled in the next few weeks, their homecoming in D.C. this weekend was enough to cast the entire city under a spell. Rare are the moments when you see the town about which "Do The Standing Still" was written carried away in collective, admittedly cheesy hand gesture, but when you're screaming along with a few hundred people at the Black Cat and you get to the part in the song that goes, "The city's been dead since you've been gone," what else is there to do but point at those four dudes on stage.

JERICHO / II ::
ACCIDENTAL SOUND

Joel Elliott
7 September 2011

On the same night when beloved NDP leader Jack Layton died and
the Libyan rebels entered Tripoli, I heard the wheels of a skateboard
roll casually off the sidewalk as if of their own accord, and I remembered a night when we walked straight down the middle of the street,
but I could not remember which night or which street.

One of the main achievements of sound in recent decades is its
ability to transform space, be it physically (from the competing
sounds of a busy shopping centre to a multimedia gallery installation) or just through the imagination that a single recording stirs up.
The above thought came to me abruptly in a hypnagogic state, as
much if not more prompted by whatever psychological state I was in
than any external factor per se.

The word "hypnagogic"—that liminal space between wakefulness
and sleep—has, with the speed of micro-genre-casting that happens
these days, become inextricably bound with David Keenan's article in
The Wire where he coined the term "hypnagogic pop." It's a brilliant
idea in principle: that melodies could be half-remembered, and thus
evoke as much the subconscious strata behind its makers as the actual
cultural touchstones referenced. In practice the latter can drown out
the former, nostalgia reduced to a set of almost compulsively-ritual-
ized tropes, bound to a specific past (the '80s, namely), and thus by

extension bound to the present in the way the Hipstamatic will never recall Polaroids as much as it will other smartphone technology in years to come. Our current brand of retro-fetishism is like a hole being dug in soft sand: the lack of stability of the present keeps leveling out any attempts to mine the past. Its culmination, as I see it, lies in bands like Washed Out: evocative of exactly nothing, a symptom of the malaise that drives escapism but not the escape itself.

But the current that drives this type of music is interesting even when the music itself fails to inspire, as a reminder that the overlap between political/cultural histories and personal histories isn't always smooth. Like the protagonist of Jiří Menzel's brilliant *Closely Watched Trains* (1966), even the most cataclysmic events can seem like a faint backdrop to the single-minded pursuits of youth. Conveniently, my generation is uniquely placed to barely -remember a decade which, according to Keenan, "seemed designed to elevate trivial feelings and everyday ups and downs to the level of tragedy," though maybe this too is a mis-remembering, and when current popular music gains its own patina it will similarly bear the "urge to excess." Sometimes, when the past is magnified to the point of distortion, new and incredible shapes emerge. When Keenan originally profiled Emeralds, I still considered them to be another in a long line of hyper-prolific cassette/CDR-format drone artists, but with last year's *Does It Look Like I'm Here?* (2010), they really did begin to sound like a "coda from an epically sad 1980s Top 40 hit extended to infinity." The gloss of sentimentality and cheap artifice that this implies can, in patient hands, become subverted by repetition until it reaches a level of transcendence that most mainstream pop from the '80s only accidentally and intermittently stumbled upon.

Generally though, the core of memory is frayed and unpredictable. Memory without noise is often a picture of some imagined notion of innocence rather than an attempt to contend with the past as past. Leyland Kirby's recent release as the Caretaker, *An Empty Bliss Beyond this World* (2011), may be the closest approximation of the more ragged type of memory ever put to tape. With a minimum of artistic intervention, Kirby still manages to completely recontextualize the dusty 78s of his source material, tracks which, even without the crackling and decay that Kirby attenuates, would evoke an almost indigestible nostalgia. And yet, his treatment is entirely counterintuitive: loops veer long past the point of comfort and into dementia, then are cut off abruptly, sometimes mid-phrase. Attempting to simulate the loss of memory in Alzheimer's sufferers, *An Empty Bliss* finds that space between recollection and eternal recurrence, emotional resonance and anonymity. Like Andrew Hall, I find the lack of a distinct creative identity behind the mix disquieting, though I also take it to be a sign of the profound absence on display. Memory soundscapes require a certain amount of relinquishing control: unsurprisingly, in a memory-obsessed culture, more and more sound artists seem to be acting as documentarians.

I recently attended Electric Eclectics, a festival near my hometown of Owen Sound, Ontario, which I reviewed a couple years back. The festival itself sometimes seems like a half-forgotten dream of noise, pop, and the avant-garde, blurred together on a beautiful rolling green hill, where torn pieces of plastic toys are nailed haphazardly to trees like a warning to children from a deranged recluse. Here, miles away from what most urbanites would consider substantial culture, someone with as much notoriety as Tony Conrad "DJ"-ed in between sets, which mostly involved playing long, unimpeded segments of audio tracks from old educational reels.

Among the performers was Canadian composer John Oswald. Oswald was effectively the bridge between musique concrète and hip-hop, and his arrangement of samples occasionally recalls both. In an essay written in 1985—five years before Michael Jackson and others threatened legal action for his unauthorized sampling of their music—he coined the term "plunderphonics" to describe his method. He asks whether there is any true distinction between sound producers (instruments) and reproducers (recordings) and why there is no equivalent in music to the literary quotation marks—a similar complaint I heard from filmmakers at a session on copyright law. Plunderphonics is a philosophy that encourages liberal use of previous recordings, including manipulating speed and playback direction, but with the important distinction of preserving the intelligibility of the original recording.

David Toop, in his brilliantly free-form exploration of music, space and memory *Haunted Weather* (2004), calls Oswald's music the "collapsing and subversion of memories," promoting an "acceptance of change and decay." As with Kirby there is a willingness to allow the inherent irrationality of memories and dreams to be preserved, and to simulate their instability. On his remix of Bing Crosby's "White Christmas" he shifts the speed subtly back and forth, as if struggling to get to the end, frantically trying to keep the orchestra from dissolving into some Edgard Varèse nightmare.

I would call this noise music in the purest sense. Its closest comparison in scope might be John Zorn's Naked City, in the way 20th century classical, jazz, cinema and pop all seem to float precariously together. In the essay, Oswald dismisses melody as the cornerstone of musical composition in favorfavour of timbre, and suggests the same goes for pop: "Notes with their rhythm and pitch values are trivial components in the corporate harmonization of cacophony." In a way, his music brings out the inherent noise of pop radio, and often his arrangements purposely thwart communication, one track remixing a reading of a mystery novel by isolating only transient words, continually setting up a scene that never happens. As in dreams, the architecture of real life seems to support nothing.

The piece recalls an installation also featured at Electric Eclectics, Christof Migone's "The Rise and Fall of the Sounds and Silences From Mars," which isolated every sound and silence-related word from Ray Bradbury's *The Martian Chronicles* (1950) onto large placards which blew in the wind. quiet. crackled. voices wailed. voices. voices. The words in print are a reminder of the sound that isn't there, but also the distinct way in which sound can be easily disembodied and wrenched from its initial meaning and context, part of an alien landscape.

R. Murray Schafer used the term "schizophonia" to refer to the division between the source of a sound and its reproduction, part of his lament for a society full of noise which drowns out natural soundscapes (a term Schafer coined and which now seems indispensable to sound culture). In many ways, "plunderphonics" is the upswing of "schizophonia," and Oswald's positioning of all sound as source seems to suggest something more democratic as well as subversive. Indeed, Schafer can seem at times autocratic, as Toop notes. His prescription for music educators was to "encourage those sounds salubrious to human life and rage against those inimical to it," without ever asking how it is determined that certain sounds are inimical, and who gets to decide.

Toop wonders if noise with its "demand to be felt" becomes perverted into a desire to understand and explain it. He also discusses the Japanese concept of shakkei, or "borrowed scenery," where all the elements outside of a controlled space—natural or man-made—become incorporated into the design. That skateboard served as a shakkei, an accidental sound that triggered both memories and the imagination of places I've never been, only remotely familiar. It's hard to imagine this kind of re-purposing without the intrusion of the unexpected.

GUCCI MANE: MY CHAIN HEAVY

Colin McGowan
23 September 2011

When I first began listening to Gucci Mane, I was living in a building with a mild cockroach problem. Living with insects is a minor affliction: a roach skitters across the kitchen floor from under the fridge; you grab a shoe, and smash the pest. It's an 8-second kind of problem—other than a little bug gunk on your loafers, nothing to fret over. But if you're the nervous type, infestation is kind of a harrowing experience. While living in this dilapidated building, cooking was a nerve-racking activity. I felt an acute rush of dread every time something small moved in my peripheral vision.

Gucci Mane's discography, were it an architectural structure, would be a mansion made out of cardboard. In this dwelling, the furniture in certain rooms would be composed entirely of roach carcasses. Some rooms would have soft-serve ice cream machines and fountains that dispense Hennessey Black. Others would possess hallucinogenic qualities. Gucci, the idiosyncratic landlord of this shithole/paradise, would sometimes invite you into his opulent living quarters to drink champagne and observe private sex shows. The next day he would threaten you at gunpoint.

Gucci Mane's mercurial, is my point, and his music is an extension of that bizarre volatility. Wrapping words around it is like trying to describe a party through photographs—the color of a person's outfit or the size of their smile is sort of irrelevant to what actually happened. Like most great artists, the high points of Gucci's oeuvre elude description, but not for obvious reasons. One might struggle to find words for, say, the title track of Funkadelic's *Maggot Brain* (1971) because of its emotional heft or the contours of William Basinski's work because it's amorphous and expands slowly like a soufflé. The components of Gucci Mane's music are easy to characterize and largely uniform: bargain basement Casio beats and couplets delivered in a slurred flow which occasionally crests, sharp and frothing. He makes masterpieces from popsicle sticks and glue, and it's at first difficult to discern how his popsicle stick sculptures are much better than anyone else's, especially when most just see a jumble of splintery wood.

People reject Gucci Mane on totally understandable terms. They see a snarling buffoon, all stupid diamond ornaments and gun talk. His rapping isn't ostensibly smart; it sometimes sounds like what a computer with hood sensibilities might spit out at random. He rhymes over production that would have sounded dated in 1998. And similar to all mixtape rappers, much of his music is marred by the incessant shouting of gatekeepers like DJ Holiday and DJ Drama, something for which fervent rap fans learn to develop a sort of Stockholm syndrome. The sensation of listening to even an exceptional Gucci Mane track is like swilling spoiled milk that tastes delicious. He is the greatest discography artist in rap if one measures discographies only in vastness, and there is nary a release in that discography with at least a track or two that doesn't greet one's eardrum like a paperclip's point. And that's before we get to the part where he talks about seducing "your girl" as if he's snatching the deed to a blowjob machine from your fingers.

In 2009, Gucci Mane released his first commercial record since excavating himself from obscurity: *The State Vs. Radric Davis*. He rarely sounds at home over major label production—the kind with actual instruments or synth patches developed before 1993—but over the piano plinks of The State's third single "Lemonade," Gucci shines as ebulliently as he does on the low-rent trilogy of Cold War mixtapes released earlier that year. One might sort-of remember that Gucci scored a big single in 2005 with "Icy," on which he sounded like an also-ran from the Cash Money camp. "Lemonade" and previous singles "Wasted" and "Spotlight" (which featured Usher) were bigger; Gucci appeared primed to vault himself into the mainstream.

As is his wont, Gucci Mane elected to fuck all of this up. In November of 2009, he was sentenced to twelve months in jail for violating the terms of the probation under which he had been placed for pleading guilty to assault in 2005. He violated his probation by completing only twenty-five hours of his court-ordered 600 hours of community service. He served only six months of his sentence.

Shortly after exiting prison, he released the "street album" *Mr. Zone 6* (2011). Were the Gucci Mane canon composed of complete documents rather than tracks cherry-picked from his yawning discography, *Mr. Zone 6* would be classified as Major Gucci. It's a stunning palette of what makes his music compelling. There are sweltering hood anthems like "You Know What It Is" and "Stove Music," each punctuated by the apoplectic yelps of his friend and foil Waka Flocka Flame. The title track exemplifies Gucci's knack for crafting songs that swirl and creep like blue smoke in a gray miasma. And at its core pulses "Georgia's Most Wanted," over which Gucci delineates his mission statement in an opening couplet: "I spend my winter in the jail, so I'm ballin' all summer / Bad bitches on my tail hunt me like a bounty hunter."

In a herculean attempt to follow that statement to the letter, Gucci was arrested in November of 2010 for a slew of traffic violations, including driving on the wrong side of the road without a license. These charges were later dropped, but Gucci still faced a possible revocation of his probation. In late December, his lawyers filed a Special Plea of Mental Incompetency, and the following month, a judge in the Superior Court of Georgia's Fulton County ordered he be sent to a psychiatric hospital. When Gucci was released from the facility later in the month, he immediately hit up a tattoo shop, and some immensely bemused artist carved a giant, three-scoop ice cream cone into his right cheek.

You might have heard about that ice cream cone tattoo. It was all over the place for a few days, chuckle-fodder for those lazily clicking around the internet during work hours. I guffawed too, but the tat story illuminates how increasingly clownish and ephemerally interesting the ATLien has grown over the past year. Snarky blogs have had fun with the eccentric rapper, but, for those not amused by his idiocy, the remainder of 2011 has been an exercise in perfunctoriness for Gucci: pop up on crew members' mixtapes and sound like lukewarm milk; drop a mediocre solo tape; shove a woman out of a moving car when she refuses to have sex with you (go to jail for that); release another mixtape that's only marginally better than the last one; be a worse rapper than Waka Flocka.

***

I eventually moved out of my ratty apartment because the insect community had begun to conspire against me. The roaches informed some bedbugs that I wasn't nervous or itchy enough, and after three months of waking up with archipelagos of red mounds on my hands and ankles, I decided it was time to dip into my bank account and find a nicer place. Bedbugs are like roaches that live in the underbelly of your heart. Or your futon, which was the only piece of furniture in my postage-stamp studio. They're just pests, ultimately—a few bug bites never hurt anyone—but their nature is unsettling. They hide in the dark corners of your possessions. They crawl on you while you sleep. They swell when they're full of blood. The whole time I was living with them, I felt unclean, like some midnight green mold was growing beneath my skin.

Gucci Mane fandom is like living with bedbugs. Fluorescent bedbugs that form intricate patterns of bites on your forearm, but still: pests. One can never be comfortable; you can't really scrub the nervous whispers from your medulla. Because his misogyny, his general idiocy, his allegiance to mixtape DJs, his inability to edit, his questionable choice in collaborators: these are all things with which you learn to live. There is no loophole in logic that can marginalize or expunge them. When Gucci releases a mixtape full of verses that reek like week-old Chinese food—as he frequently has over the past twelve months, capping off his run of mediocrity by being subsumed by Waka Flocka on the duo's *Ferrari Boyz* (2011)—one must digest it and suffer the gastrointestinal consequences. A Gucci fan doesn't eat their vegetables; they eat the grease-soaked junk no one should. We do this, lamentably, because he lives in the underbelly of our hearts.

Gucci was once less irksome. Funnier, too. For how marble-mouthed and obfuscated by slang his bars are, they possess some sharp moments of humor. "Cowards and Soldiers" is supposed to be about how he murders people, but it begins with the line "My traphouse just like Morehouse: I got niggas all around it," which is a funny historically black college joke, one around which Gucci crafts an entire verse, turning references to sororities and Spelman College over themselves like an axleless wheel tumbling downhill. And in the second verse he sarcastically characterizes his coke as "whiter than Taylor Swift." The wheel keeps sputtering along, and he never actually gets around to gun talk.

He can also spend unbroken hours talking about little else than things that are shiny, black, loud, and violent. Or he talks about himself. The main conceit of Gucci Mane's oeuvre is Gucci Mane, and he is all of those things. We know this because he compulsively sings himself all over chintzy synths and 808 ticks, over volumes and volumes of mixtapes, like a rapidly dying memoirist. Over (literally) days worth of music, Gucci sketches some sort of topographical map of himself, coloring in every dollar bill and drawing cartoonish lightning bolts around his nihilism. The map is, in various spots, terrifying, uninteresting, and gorgeous, but the whole thing is rendered in the hazy filter of his perverse grasp of the English language. Gucci's music arrives to one's ears like the bending, shifting light from a celestial body. I'm not sure—even after sifting through dozens of releases—that I know Gucci, but I definitely know things about him. (He's temperamental, for example.) And I only care to learn about him because he talks about Gucci Mane like no one else can.

Gucci's greatest asset has always been his absurd, carnivorous relationship with language. His best tracks are like watching an artist paint with the brush clutched between his toes. On OJ Da Juiceman's "Make The Trap Say Aye," he unfurls this garbled chain of sound: "I'm twerkin' birds in so we workin' / Packin' a truck stop to train a back in / We big flip jug; we tote it off the forklift / The way my plug kick ya think he had a black belt." He's talking about cocaine trafficking, but then Springsteen was just talking about factory workers. Dope boys are hip-hop's factory workers.

So, Gucci Mane takes genre tropes with which rap fans are comfortable, even bored, and haphazardly reassembles them. He builds familiar structures out of LEGOs, but instead of snapping blocks together, he melts and distorts the blocks and builds a skyscraper out of irregular hexagons. He does this like it's the most normal thing in the world.

I remember a specific episode of *MTV Cribs* in which Lil Wayne was showing off a chain that featured a gigantic, iced-out New Orleans Hornets logo. It was a mesmerizingly stupid piece of jewelry. The hip-hop universe is littered with these ugly, luminescent things: Gucci himself has a Bart Simpson chain; Rick Ross frequently wears one modeled after his own face; even a talentless moron like Plies has a diamond-encrusted pendant shaped like a skimask-clad goon. If you have ever attended a rap show, you have also realized these sparkly status symbols are sort of hypnotic. In the correct lighting, one has a small epiphany: the guy on stage is wearing a $300K magnet around his neck, and it is very, very shiny.

Gucci Mane doesn't just drape these expensive ornaments over his clothes, he embodies them on a metaphysical level. He is the personification of one of hip-hop's emblems—the Rapper's Gaudy Chain made skin, ink, muscles, and flow. He is at once disgusting, troublesome, and brilliant. And sometimes just one of those things. One of Gucci's stickier hooks—from chain anthem "Excuse Me"—is an incantation that begins with facetious apology: "Please pardon me, please pardon me / I'm sorry I'm so sparkly." It's chain talk, and, by extension, Gucci talk. The grossest, shiniest talk.

JERICHO / IV ::
NOISE, TRAUMA, & RESISTANCE
(PART 1)

Joel Elliott
14 November 2011

"If the Iraqis aren't used to freedom, then I'm glad to be part of their exposure."
-James Hetfield, on the use of "Enter Sandman" in Guantánamo Bay detention camp

I always wake up to CBC Radio, and am usually still half-asleep by the time *The Current* starts at 8:30 am, bringing all the detritus of the day from around the globe and into my bedroom, interfering and intermingling with my dreams until I wake up with a thousand problems that make whatever I have to accomplish that day seem insignificant. This particular morning fell about a week before the tenth anniversary of 9/11, and the program replayed the live on-air reactions to the second tower being hit, that eerie pull every news-caster faced between reacting to the horror and trying to narrate the events to the audience, to meet both the requirements of being human and the requirements of being a journalist. Radio being the best conduit for false panic (remember Orson Welles' *War Of The Worlds* (1938) fiasco?), I was convinced this was happening in real time, the spontaneous moment of visceral reaction reliving itself over again, like an Alzheimer's patient suffering through the death of a spouse day after day.

As if that wasn't bad enough, later in the day I was standing in my kitchen when I felt my entire third-floor Toronto apartment shake. Not being overly familiar with protocol in these situations, I jumped into the corner behind the fridge and put my hands over my head. As it turns out, the Canadian National Exhibition wasn't going to let a little bad timing interfere with its annual airshow.

As ridiculous as these responses were, I feel like the last decade has been one of similarly manufactured trauma—a parody of fear, though I wouldn't tell that to anyone with a poor heart condition unfortunate enough to be living somewhere near the flyover, or someone with a good reason to be traumatized by that kind of display of military strength. I wondered if my Afghan neighbours from my old house out on the Danforth felt that roar, and what their reaction might be, especially if they hadn't lived here long enough to fully absorb the unique way terror and entertainment serve as reflections of each other in our culture.

Louis Althusser wrote that one of the chief characteristics of ideology was that of masking its own operations, so that its perspectives seemed natural. In the same way, the replaying of those towers falling was made to seem natural—stoic even, part of our collective responsibility—rather than compulsive, as two deeply embroiled wars needed to be continually re-cast as retaliatory and urgent. Thus even those far removed geographically from the disaster were allowed to share in its collective trauma.

Ironically, the event would stimulate a war where noise became a guiding principle. The concept of "shock and awe" went from a vague principle of intimidation to a coherent strategy. The idea that the military needed to use less overtly physical, subtler weapons was built into both the technology of modern warfare and the nature of counterinsurgency. Retired US Air Force Lt-Col Dan Kuehl, who teaches psychological operations at the National Defence University in Washington DC, even referenced the battle of Jericho when talking to the St. Petersburg Times: "His men might not have been able to break down literal walls with their trumpets, but the noise eroded the enemy's courage."

The use of music as torture at Guantanamo Bay became the most notorious instance of organized noise in the last decade, though probably more than anything as a result of the variety of music used: everything from Metallica and Deicide to the "I Love You" song from Barney & Friends. Bob Singleton, the writer of "I Love You," seemed more incredulous (if perhaps slightly embarrassed) than outraged: "A song that was designed to make little children feel safe and loved was somehow going to threaten the mental state of adults and drive them to the emotional breaking point?", he wrote to the LA Times. His designation of "music is just music" ignores the fact that music played at excessively loud volumes for hours and days at a time induces an incredible amount of psychological damage.

Former Gitmo inmate Binyam Mohamed told human rights lawyer Clive Stafford Smith that he had faced a razor blade to his penis continually for 18 months while incarcerated in Morocco, and American "psyops" were worse, because you could anticipate the end of physical pain in a way you couldn't with psychological damage. Elaine Scarry defines torture as an attempt to "unmake the world" of the detainee: in this case, by exposing Middle Eastern inmates who might otherwise have little direct experience of American culture to the most vacuous and grating music it has to offer. The irony may have been lost on the guards responsible for "breaking" prisoners: it's not difficult to imagine the same heavy metal records scoring treks into warzones, adrenaline and fear being similar emotions with similar triggers.

The difference is context, and to ignore context is to ignore that point where music becomes noise (of the deleterious kind), where not only is the music beyond the recipient's control, but its entire function is to make the recipient aware of his own helplessness. Incidentally, loss of control is central to definitions of post-traumatic stress disorder, particularly as defined by Judith Herman in her landmark study Trauma & Recovery, linking trauma and noise in an eternal braid of despair and helplessness. There's even a yet-to-be-officially-recognized term for the type of prolonged exposure to traumatic situations constituted by torture: "complex post-traumatic stress disorder," which distinguishes itself from ordinary PTSD mainly by a level of psychological fragmentation that results in a loss of a "coherent sense of self." In addition to music, the guards apparently also employed recordings of babies with colic. A convenient metaphor: the sound of helplessness, of inexplicable, pertinacious suffering, to produce the same effect in the prisoners.

The above quote is a succinct reminder that the culture which confuses a 14-year-old boy annoying his parents by blasting "Enter Sandman" with a prisoner in a cell being forced to listen to the same at ear-splitting volumes for days on end (and often followed by equally agonizing sensory deprivation and silence) is the same one which imagines "freedom" to be a set of rigidly coded values and symbols as opposed to a condition of being. It reminds me of the '50s, when the CIA funded concerts featuring the work of serialist composers like Pierre Boulez and Milton Babbitt for an ideological war against the Soviet Union that was nearly as phantasmal as the belief that a severely damaged psyche produces good intelligence. I like Serialism and I don't care for Metallica, but stuffing twelve-tone-rows down the shirts of Eastern bloc composers seems like a milder precursor to audio torture.

Then there's Steve Ashiem of Deicide, whose "Fuck Your God" was a Gitmo favorite: "If I was a prisoner at Guantánamo Bay and they blasted a load of music at me, I'd be like, 'Is this all you got? Come on.' They are warriors and they're trained to resist torture." It's a similar argument used on our own traumatized soldiers: it seems blaming the victim is as old as trauma itself, from rape victims to the Armenians who suffered genocide under the Ottoman Turks nearly a century ago. Herman explicitly positioned her definition of trauma as a challenge to the social and political status quo: "the most traumatic events … take place outside the realm of socially validated reality." But the effects of noise and trauma, while invisible, are as real as physical wounds: I met an ex-Canadian Forces corporal whose entire platoon suffered PTSD after a tour in Bosnia, as if a psychological land mine had gone off in the middle of them. Its triggers are often aural, and occasionally unexpected: the same veteran told me another soldier had complained to him about his counsellor clicking a pen repeatedly, which brought back memories of an IED being set off.

What is the relationship between noise and trauma, besides an intensely internal and invisible, but concrete, scarring? As in that ex-prisoner's testimony, both seem to go on forever without an anticipated end: when the noise stops, the psychological reverberations echo indefinitely. As in elevator music—that most unobtrusive form of noise—they are made to be constant, to envelop a space and to drown out either silence or rational thought. Any sounds played loud enough would serve this purpose, though certain kinds of heavy metal seem strangely appropriate: how ironic is it that Metallica's later albums have been at the forefront of the so-called "loudness wars," the over-compression and dynamic flattening so characteristic of mainstream rock records in the last two decades? Even the waveform from *Death Magnetic* (2008) seems to want to consume the entire space it's in.

TALK TALK: LAUGHING STOCK

Chet Betz
4 November 2011

It's kind of hard for me to talk about Talk Talk. I remember, years ago, friend and colleague Eric Sams asked me to my face how I could say that *Spirit of Eden* (1988) and *Laughing Stock* (1991) are my two favorite albums of all time (I put *Laughing Stock* on top but can't really separate the two), and I think I managed a few sentences before choking back something that felt like my soul. Though it's the opposite of what we usually strive for here at the Glow, think of this review as a recommendation, not a piece of actual criticism. The latter would take me more than a minute. And probably more than typing.

If the six-song cycle of *Spirit of Eden* creates a metaphysical subtext for the book of Genesis, then the six-song cycle of *Laughing Stock* is a jump cut forward to the New Testament (c'mon, "Myrrhman"? "Ascension Day"?) and beyond. There's still that connection between "The Rainbow" and "After the Flood," the parallel drawn cross-testament to God's greatest promises of hope to man, and then the sublime "New Grass" brings us to a summit to look down on a verdant valley with a New Jerusalem. And we look with new eyes, new skin and flesh on our bones, a regenerated soul stirring within. I'm not exaggerating. For me art at its highest is like this, this insightful deconstruction of the myths that bind us, delineating the essential from the literal; it is the most true arc of the spiritual, the launching point being all of our origins and the stories thereof, the leap from that basis being a bold stab into the heart of the unknown—our inmost selves. For while it's a gross understatement to say that the cosmos dwarf us and our supposed significance, they may also serve as a universal mirror of some divine spark within us. In cinema Tarkovsky was rigorous in expressing these ideas through various narratives and symbols while shrouding them in an ambiguity, an awe-filled mystery that was as honest as the truths he underlined. In music I'd say Mark Hollis, the head of Talk Talk, is the closest equivalent.

And there's an emotional heft here that shouldn't be slept on. Every time I hear Mark Hollis cry out, offering up his freedom in thanks for "a sacred love" on *Spirit of Eden* closer "Wealth," there's a calm elation—like slowly waking to a brilliant sunbeam pulsing through a crack in the blinds. Every time I hear the long sigh of that solemn sustain—an unexpected murmur of wind—at the end of *Laughing Stock* opener "Myrrhman," tears pool. The tapestry this music weaves is rife with iconography, knowing that the iconic when rendered with great artistry has a resonance that can level all cognitive and cultural barriers.

In many ways Tarkovsky's technique and aesthetic defined his content; he was an absolute master of the long-take and this mastery was part and parcel with his philosophy of "sculpting in time" as the fullest potential of filmmaking. In similar fashion Talk Talk's music possesses a sort of incomparable patience and fluidity; I think we tend to think of music as an art possessing great inherent continuity with its flow of overlapping components—and Talk Talk's last two albums are the exceptional examples that expose the lie in our perception. Even the best electronica sounds like it's playing techno Tetris with Pro Tools blocks compared to these long-form analog compositions that intertwine their threads delicately, finding integrity in a sort of vulnerability while also managing to play off of and subvert traditional song structures and dynamics, pinching music theory on the cheek or even pulling it by the ear (one-note guitar solo, anyone?). Tim Friese-Greene's production is immaculate, each sound distinct, rich, and purely fertile in the way it pushes the compositions to develop without becoming entangled or overgrown messes.

The end results are songs that can't be called tracks but maybe then not even "songs," if songcraft really is all about creating lil' self-contained works meant to emphasize strong melodies and/or lyrical wit. Instead, Talk Talk show us how they walk their walk, not just talk it; the very grace of their music's movement demonstrates that pits and plateaus don't always lead to peaks (but sometimes), that life can often seem static when it actually defies stasis through the elegance of the cyclical and the elliptical ("Taphead," holy shit), and that we can exist in the moment but only insomuch as we realize that the moment is simultaneously ephemeral and eternal.

Reduction, refraction, reincarnation of the music canon is a symptom of this lean on recurrence; whole genres are mere chromosomes in Talk Talk's DNA. In Lee Harris' drums there rumbles jazz whittled down into cretacean backbones; in the music's preternatural feel for use of negative space lies a sensibility to rival the best of the avant-garde; in its symphonic compositions a minimalist approach to classicist grandeur, epitomizing the 20th century and its trends towards dissonance and modality; in its sound editing and post-production arrangement a prescience for hip-hop and electronica; in the variety and reach of its instrumentation a sort of concentrated, Europe-centric world music; in its blasts of harmonica the roots of blues; in its keys, ambient; and with its guitar comes a keen understanding of the power of the occasional bit of distortion. There is also cowbell and it rocks, absolutely. Mark Hollis' tremulous voice carries the aching sentiment of pop music; his words read like the most poetic and cryptic of Scriptures, displaced in time by Renaissance and relativity. The organism this DNA creates is of its sources transcendent, a term I'll now retire in my music criticism as I realize that no record really deserves "transcendent" the way these records do. But there's so much to this music that no terminology can really hope to touch.

"Can't put into words" is always a cop-out but know that beneath this (relatively) scant writing lies a massive number of things that go unsaid, what feels like a lifetime of listening to these records and being moved by them to a place beyond words. And yet we go on trying to find some way to express the ineffable. This is why a masterpiece like *Laughing Stock*, my bona fide favorite album ever, exists in the first place. If the music of the spheres is the ideal, Talk Talk's final records and the Mark Hollis solo album are the music of the immediate matter touched by those spheres, the gleaming dark in between, irradiated into beautiful, broken harmony—trying to speak of something that can't be spoken. You, listener, have a choice: admire this music from afar … or really open up to it and allow the glow it reflects to seep into your pores. Listen to this music and be impressed, or listen to this music and be transformed. I recommend the latter.

JENNY HVAL:
VISCERA

Mark Abraham
From CMG's Best Albums of 2011 list

I've always been fascinated by the body as an academic pursuit, but having spent 2011 recovering from the surgery required to remove a benign hemanginoma tumor from my spine I've had a far more intimate experience with my own body this past year. "I came back with a broken spine." Pain, sure, and aches and stiffness, but also how peeing is affected, say, by losing a half inch of height. Or the strange knot I have just below my left breast that is probably the result of a severed nerve. Or the drowsy pleasure of Morphine, Fentanyl, Oxycodone, and Codeine. What it's like to wake up after a 12-hour surgery in a room you've never seen before, your face puffy as fuck, "from my veins … a strange itching," and, seeing the mixture of relief and concern on loved ones' faces, your own reaction is basically, "so … how was everyone's day?" Or how my legs, which stopped working last November, are working now, but still kind of feel like I can't quite totally feel them working. Or how a rib that was removed in surgery affects my posture. "Tried yoga. Couldn't do yoga." Even simple things, like how many times I'll have to readjust my back while writing this blurb, or how I hope the dog doesn't wander off with mischief in mind because it takes me a full 10 seconds to get off the couch and stand erect. Which … doesn't seem like a lot of time, I know, but count how many seconds it takes those of you who haven't had major spine surgery to get up. People ask me how I am, and I say "basically normal," but it's hard to explain what "basically normal" is exactly like.

Viscera (2011) obviously isn't about my body, but bodies are its preoccupation, both because Hval's lyrics focus on them and because her songs are sewn together like thick, out-of-order mannequin parts. These are sinewy tracks; they have a bend to them; they are littered with synecdoches and metonyms for ineffable truths that are only meaningful to individuals: "my humming is my own." When Hval says "we share thighs but not languages," she cuts to the carnality that unites all humans across the socially constructed boxes we've constructed for each other. But this carnality, teeth and all, shouldn't be mistaken simply for sex; it's true that Hval opens the album with a line about stimulating her clitoris with an electric toothbrush, but the imagery is just as much about robots and organisms as it is about rubbing and orgasm—it's about the frailty of the body as an engine as much as it is about training ourselves to experience the pleasure that our bodies can provide. Which is not to take away from Hval's wielded sexuality—this album is feminist, and the reactions her frankness has gotten in some quarters suggests female sexuality is still strangely knotty for certain parties—but is simply to say that it isn't only feminist, or only concerned with women. It's an album about how our bodies share languages, waste, and direction; it's only how we interpret these things that is our own. It's focused on internal synapses, and not external signifiers. "The body is a one-way street." "The body remembers." "This is where I come from." All true; all universal; all pointing to the way we physically experience the shit our brain organizes and unveils for us. 'Cause we're all still basically babies, or like the dog sitting next to me; running off to chew things is the first way we experience the world, and speech, in the world of *Viscera*, an album so fascinated with passing things mouth to mouth, is merely an evolution of that action.

It's easy to get caught up in the poetics, I think, because for all the jaw drops at Hval's vagina dentata reference her actual lyricism is quite restrained. It's vague enough for us to take our own meanings from it (the title track, for example, seems to perfectly describe my painful week immediately after my surgery, trying but failing to talk eloquently about anything), but just pointed enough to make a simple case for the validity of the body as an organizing principle for humanity. But what makes *Viscera* an Album of the year and not just a Collection of Poems Set To Music of the year is the way Hval and her bandmates and producer (Supersilent's Deathprod) take the body as a point of departure for song construction: there are no real verses or choruses on Viscera, because an elbow isn't a chorus. Hval instead speaks "body and bone," tracing the "wet line" of spines and ribs and hair through her music.

It's not surprising, maybe, that her aesthetic is partially a marriage of maritime-ish folk and industrial noise: this is an album about traveling the body, and the ships and trains that connect our organs and joints are wet and rigid. It's kind of astonishing how confident this aesthetic is, actually. We could point to stylistic touchstones— folk gods like Tim Buckley, Joni Mitchell, Kate Bush, Mary Margaret O'Hara, Fairport Convention, and the McGarrigles—but the weight of the music is Hval's own. It's expansive, enveloping; it feels modeled on the way a body falls at rest, the arrangements fixating on pores, wayward hairs, fingernails, and sleep dirt. The songs start at the fingers and toes with simple guitar plucks but the music soars as we crest shoulders and thighs and get a clear view of the landscape. Seaweed, oceans, trains, fingers, hands, and ribs. Things that connect and things that entangle. Sex isn't just sex; it's another way our bodies speak to one another. Breast milk isn't just marrow; it's veins and words and secrets. It's all shit that binds us together, is the overwhelming message. We can speak to one another when we choose, but *Viscera* is beautiful in its recognition that our bodies constantly are.

JERICHO / IV :: NOISE, TRAUMA & RESISTANCE (PART 2)

Joel Elliott
28 February 2012

Conscious sonic environments are an antidote, in terms of both space and time: one of the most prominent achievements of sound art was to bracket off noise with some form of beginning and ending. As if to combat my own irritation at the constant flyovers, I decided to go down to the waterfront to record sounds from the airshow. David Toop noted that the sound of loud airplanes is probably one of the least interesting or dynamic noises you can hear, reduced to a constant Doppler effect (hence why everyone goes to a stock car race hoping for a crash, anything to break out of that mindless drone), but somehow I felt compelled to record it anyway. Perhaps concentrating on something through a camera lens or headphones reduces its power to irritate. Playing it back and stopping it at will transforms it into a creative act rather than an external assault.

This is how Toop describes the attacks on the World Trade Center: "Unlike the satisfyingly tidy impact and 'closure' of a Hollywood explosion, the sounds heard on television rolling news as the towers collapsed were fragmented, seemingly boundless…" He asked Lee Ranaldo, who lives with his family near Ground Zero, to describe his sonic experience of that morning. After hearing both planes hit, he took the elevator to the rooftop of his apartment building. What he heard initially sounded like more planes attacking, but vaguely and indescribably different, a giant, unidentifiable roaring noise. Only when he returned to his apartment and saw the black smoke on his television and forming around his window did he realize he'd witnessed the sound of the towers about to crumble.

When I emailed Ranaldo to ask him more about the noise he stopped short of admitting New York itself was traumatized by the sound, though he did admit that the city's sounds, so integral to the development of volume-centric artists like Glenn Branca, Swans, and Sonic Youth themselves, were both "inspiring" and at times "over-whelming."

In the past several months, there's been a different kind of noise on the streets. I don't think it's a coincidence that Occupy Wall Street arose a decade after September 11th, what Time called the "worst decade since World War II," ten years that most North Americans seemed to sleepwalk through, either blind by cynicism or patriotic fervor. If America wasn't traumatized, it at least shared some of the same characteristics: it seemed incapable of joining the present.

One of the most integral effects of the movement was to disrupt this sense of being on autopilot: it may not have won over a lot of people who weren't already fed up with big banks and corporate oligarchy, but it did manage to make them re-think possible models of resistance. It wasn't just a protest, but a form of living in protest, and in that sense aimed to engage with the very day-to-day existential hole that most people in neoliberal countries had found themselves.

Ranaldo has been very active in Occupy Wall Street, both document-ing it on his website and even employing audio recordings in his work. For Toronto's Avant X Festival, he collaborated with his wife, video artist Leah Singer, on a piece called Contre Jour. The piece is one of many permutations of his "swinging guitar" technique, a heavily effects-laden electric guitar attached by a rope to the ceiling, which he alternately bangs with a drumstick or bow and sends revolving around the room, creating subtle, rhythmic shifts in feedback and sustained tone, conceptually not unlike Steve Reich's "Pendulum Music" (which Sonic Youth performed for their SYR release *Goodbye 20th Century* [1999]). The whole thing has a rather satisfying mix of rock 'n' roll's theatricality and conceptual art's minimalist gestures in a way that seems to epitomize the history of New York's underground art scene.

Singer's accompanying still images and videos (which were on an even larger scale for a previous performance at Toronto's Nuit Blanche) tend to combine the minute with the panoramic, creating a poetry of broad gestures. Her images seem to pulsate light even when static, and Ranaldo's guitar sometimes carries the impression of swinging right into the landscape depicted and getting swallowed in a sunspot; an effect even more heightened when a pure flicker on the screen was combined with a strobe light in the room.

In one image, a crowd at a concert (Sonic Youth?) is doubled like a breaking wave. Likewise, as the chants from Occupy Wall Street enter, they are mostly unintelligible, but formed like some massive natural force. In a deafening climax (and another nod to OWS), drummers and other noisemakers hidden in the small audience began standing up and joining in, which mirrored again the dissolving of the distinctions between audience and performer, spectator and participant.

Ranaldo kept using the word "spontaneous" in referencing both the audience participation and the creation of protest songs at OWS. This is perhaps the key common thread that runs through both improvised music and 21st century grassroots action: the way both seem to emerge without a single cause, leader, or (at least in the case of OWS) clearly delineated goal. Toop talks about the theory of the "rhizome" as proposed by Gilles Deleuze and Félix Guattari: like certain plants, the model of the rhizome resists hierarchical structure and embraces lateral movement. It cannot be separated or reduced to individual components or entities. The model is typically applied to internet communities, and in the case of improvisation, digital music, but it clearly goes back to at least the '60s when free jazz gradually shed its reliance on central themes and motifs and began to hinge on moment-to-moment interactions.

In the case of political organization, few movements have embraced rhizomatic organization as completely as Occupy. My experience at Occupy Toronto saw not only a lack of identifiable central organization, but a system of checks and balances—some more effective than others—designed to create revolving-door roles, continually expanding committees and sub-committees, and a vigilante self-examination of embedded privilege and power.

Sound is an integral dimension here, most notably because of the "people's mic": the echoing of everything a speaker says by the rest of the group. Not without good reason, the tactic has been criticized as inefficient and unnecessary (as has many of Occupy's strategies), but as a model of this kind of political organization it provides a way of marking how well the group is actively participating in the process. When the assembly dissolves into noise (when a speaker speaks without waiting for the echo or when someone interrupts), it's a sign the system is coming unglued. Cries of "mic check" are attempts to restore some semblance of order: in aural terms, they are the testing of levels, the tuning up of a giant political instrument.

In this sense, noise is both a frequent means of breaking through the imposed silence of a stagnant political process, as well as the description of the spaces where the movement threatens to deteriorate and is forced to re-evaluate itself, where power seeps through the cracks. Are the two mutually exclusive? Maybe not: the energy of a rally can seep negatively into the gritty business of trying to make the difficult decisions necessary in running a kind of micro-society (as a side note, anyone who thinks the Occupiers are lazy freeloaders never went down there to see how sleep-deprived and stressed the most active organizers really were). But the risk of this dissolution is necessary in the same way that the dissent which created the Occupy movement in the first place is necessary: a little bit of chaos is proof that the group is still made up of individual human beings with differing opinions.

As much as the noise was necessary, so was the silence: I witnessed a poignant wordless march through the financial district of Toronto to the front of the TD Building where protesters simply sat with signs and handed out small flyers, reducing the concept of an "occupation" to a kind of zen-like minimum. The effect it has on the soundscape of the city is kind of incredible: sympathetic to the cause or not, the whole area around King and Bay seemed to open up an aural space. The squeak of breaks from a city bus or the clack of heels on the sidewalk, like the echo of feet in an empty cathedral or a cough in a darkened theatre before the film starts, don't so much disturb the silence as grow out of it.

And then fade back into it again.

INTERLUDE:
FAKE WEEKND LYRICS

Staff

"Often, often, girl I do this often / Invade that pussy like an ice planet, my spermtroopers they be Hoth-in"

"bring the drugs baby, I'll bring T-Pain"

"girl; puddin'; work"

"Often often, girl I do this often / A healthy and responsible sex life makes my dick soften."

"Often, often, girl I do this often / Often often often girl girl girl girl often."

"Often, often, girl I do this often / Like that Young Pope, I smoke, cigs got me coughin" - "Young Pope"

"Often, often, girl I do this often / Steve Harvey lookin' awkward, worse than Tarkin, Grand Moffin'"

"Tryna put u in a church pew ah/ Mitre cleaner than ur church shoes ah/ Look what u've done/ I'm a muthafuckin Young Pope"

"Often often, girl I do this often / if your body is your house you know I make it fuller, Lori Loughlin"

"Often often, girl I do this often / chips ahoy in the microwave, yummier when it's softened"

"I'm into poop now / And how / That's my new vow: / Poop now" ("Poop Is My New Drug")

"Often, often, girl I do this often / I don't need a mic, just your ear to jerk off in"

"Often often, #grammy winnin often / gonna take all sense of shame, bury it in a coffin"

"I can feel my face, woof, like times two / Because of the drugs, they're ruining my face...it really hurts."

"Often, often, girl I do this often / By 'this' I mean a Butt Party / Girl, let's have a Butt Party."

"Often, often, girl I do this often / Make the sex with a lady, I'm not gay *coughin*"

"She says Gaspar Noe / I say Gaspar Yes / Masturbating like a French auteur all over her new dress"

"Got my album dropping on NPR / baby dropping on PBR / DMT, girl, is where we are / coca-cola areola" - "Coca Cola Areola"

"Zomby in a Guy Fawkes mask / Fawking that zombie ass"

"Seminole seminar / Seminole seminar / In not long not long / Bring out the free bagels" - "Native American Conference"

"Adjust your webcam / Girl, I need to see all of you / Damn, your room is small / But I like your bed" - "Skype Naked"

"Shaking some Old Bay on our lobster rolls 4 breakfast / Girls cracking crabs & prawns, 1/4 to 7"

"Girl I'm right outside / I'm right outside your door / Watching you eat a bowl of ice cream." -The Weeknd, "Futons"

"Open your mouth, take the crust / ...Trust me girl, you'll wanna eat pie for this." - "Meringue"

"Drinking Alize without cereal for breakfast / Risking ulceration and potentially sepsis." - "The Morning Redux"

"Egg hunt, mama / Then 'Game of Thrones' and a sauna" - "Easter"

"Girl, I'm down with what yer grippin / Just let me select what yer sippin / Let me collect all yer drippin" - "Bed Pans"

SCHOOLBOY Q: HABITS & CONTRADICTIONS

Kaylen Hann
4 April 2012

Patios, pistachios, Portishead, and "my pursuit of happiness." With this second release from LA's hedonistic and occasionally ham-fisted rapper, ScHoolboy Q is rampantly chasing down the latter. As in previous full-length *Setbacks* (2011), there is a signature enthusiasm that blusters through this mixtape/LP hybrid, like a magnificent exhale of smoke as grating and grainy as it is intoxicating. Or: as mesmerizing as it is mightily skunked with whiffs of frankly, shockingly masterful bullshit. And, to nothing but its benefit, *Habits & Contradiction*s (2012) is a beautifully, beautifully, bullshitty piece of work.

Despite Q's driving zeal all borderline uncool in its loose-lipped "fuckity, fuck, fuck" verbiage, he raps at the sluggish pace of someone slow-burning away the dog days—maybe it's a brisk canter at its most spritely? ScHoolboy Q won't be hurried along, I mean, made to scrutinize or compromise, and as such, nothing about *Habits & Contradictions* is strictly nailed down or conveys at any point there's pressure for anything to be nailed down. CMG's Sr. Wiz Khalifa Correspondent, Colin McGowan, described Q: "Like Wiz Khalifa if Wiz were less about champagne and airplanes and more about rough sex and 40s." In other words, *Habits & Contradictions* has an unfocused focus. It's free to drift, thematically and specifically into shrugging non-sequiturs; it wields few dire moments (despite the opening track's weighted notes of arm-wrestling virtue and vices with the ponderous noodling of a western guitar); it carries no crosses bulkier than you could shoulder; it shines no harsh lights. If anything, it'd look at you like you're an asshole if you walked in and hit the switch.

Still, *Habits & Contradictions* is a pleasurable listen with head-scratchingly pretty samplings and lyrics more or less liberated from value care of Q's devotion to "weed and brews" and the delirious enjoyment of something so simple as saying "fuck" a lot. I mean: a lot, and very pointedly. It is with a spluttering joy in that particular self-indulgence that Q pronounces, "Uhhh, muthafucka', muthafucka' yeah / Fuckin' is my favorite word, reason why I'm fuckin' her," accompanied by an equally puerile leer of "Up in ya braaaaaa" on the falsetto-ish chorus for "There He Go." Which is rapped over, of all things, the tender piano palpitations of Menomena's "Wet and Rusting."

A reservoir of iniquity, salaciously effective pick-up lines, extraordinary negligence, and just … fucking awful advice (all the drunk driving, for instance), Q's lyrics really hone in on and own the "simple pleasures" sweet spot. He emerges as a Norman Rockwell scamp-figure of hip-hop's unabashedly carefree, fritterin' youth—think, like, A$AP Rocky's slightly less cool cousin? And, in a track that reads like a menu or manifesto for ardent substance abuse (with the added delight of breaks-squealing onomatopoeias: RRrr!), "Hands On The Wheel" allows related personalities room to play off one another. With Q's hardheaded "fuck"s and all-capsed "TOO DAMN HIGH" drawling out before A$AP's double-time rapping about everything that goes into a haphazard blend they've whimsically named "Pikachu," the song is easily the best on the album, doing the best job of underscoring how Q may not be the most nimble or cogent rapper, but how that's what winds up being his most impactful aspect.

Because: it honestly isn't noteworthy in itself that the lyrics are often of self-interest, then of complete egoism. The pleasure derived from them doesn't have much to do with linguistic specificity. He's Jeezy-like in that way (though un-Jeezy-like in a lot of other ways); he brandishes a Black Flag sort of rap. He's rapping about pussy and getting high in the same way Black Flag made music about depression, and he isn't bothered with the poetics. "You get it. Here's a verse that sounds like punching."

If anything perseveres, it is his unapologetic way of grabbing up whatever he feels like. "You got some pretty legs 'n shit. You should fuck with me." To blatantly quote Colin, again: "He's the dude who hits on girls at parties by being balls-out confident enough to be like 'we're sleeping together.' And you're like, 'I mean, I have reservations, but you're still not wrong.'" He basically even gets away with fucking other guys' girlfriends completely unscathed because they wind up being fans of his. Oily sidesteps and the brushing off of narrow escapes saturate the tracks as they mull around with their own sumptuous brand of aimlessness. Q has a gun, but he doesn't wind up having to use it; he has muscle, but even while, on "Raymond 1969," "murder murder murder kill" blasts from the increasingly diabolical tones of Portishead's lush, rupturing distortion, what isn't conveyed in enunciation is conveyed when Q simply steps aside and lets Beth Gibbons' vocals bare its teeth for him.

Habits & Contradictions is, then, engulfed in freedom: to use people and substances for pleasure with un-wincing consistency that gives his most juvenile sentiments a manly ring, articulated in such an insular way it weirdly enough comes off almost worldly. Insular, because much about what he's pursuing is held in some realm of pure potential. For instance, while there is sex, it is often something at arms' length. He watches someone undress, he retrospectively muses about a girl having "never been with a G" before, he sexts, and he sexts about sexting about that girl and that someone. These people are often just blurry imprints, "the girls with the heels / preferably the ones with the ass," indistinctive but utterly guaranteed. The ease with which his rhythm relates those guarantees, it's hard not to be just as drunk on that sense of possibility, which: is so fucking possible it reads as inevitable.

Curiously, it's in "Blessed" (featuring 2011's Top Dawg Entertainment breakout rapper Kendrick Lamar), which begins to pick at his past (in a way similar to *Setbacks*), that reinforces his narrow lyrical focus. While it has every potential to wield emotional weight and pathos for a rapper who normally avoids giving us that, what it mostly does is manage to eschew contradiction, and instead draw a straight, simple line from hardships—like living out of a backpack—to the way he raps unapologetically about pleasure. Q's strongest when he doesn't succumb to nostalgia or pensive pitfalls, but the lyrics in "Blessed" swing from affectingly specific images about uneven pockets ("I was hangin' on them corners late / Pockets wasn't straight, bitch") to unexpectedly humble ("I know the world got more problems and it's much bigger/ But I figured, I'd get some shit up off my chest").

It's with that kind of perspective and sincerity that Q seems to shake off dour imagery faster than it can get depressing. Like in "Sacrilegious," where he confesses to keeping "homies on shuffle," as soon as the lyrics tip towards heartache or some gesture for sympathy they recoil with a bout of optimism ("Don't stress"), followed by Q resolutely fist-bumping himself ("Ones for the money, two for the bitches / Three to get ready cause I feel I finally did it") or switching to someone else's woes as a means to appreciate what he has. And for the woeful he offers condolences, weed, whatever he's got, plus a dose of probably more bad advice, but with hopefulness. Honestly, for a guy who doesn't keep friends, he is really willing to be a heck of a pal to everyone else. Which is evident in just how comfortable he's made featured rappers like Lamar.

Habits & Contradictions is a compellingly free album, if freedom is the assurance and the power to subject each person to one's own whims, will, and wishes. And to just absolutely know he'll get what he wants. He "might crip tonight"; he "might fuck tonight"; the world is ScHoolboy Q's oyster. Just as long as what it has to offer him doesn't, y'know, get its pussy on his car seat. He explicitly does not want that.

SWANS: THE SEER

Joel Elliott
From CMG's Best Albums of 2012 list

Editor's note: In 2016, the singer-songwriter Larkin Grimm accused Swans lead Michael Gira of rape. This was four years after the release of The Seer *and the writing of this essay. Swans, as a musical entity, were a favorite of CMG, and inspired some of the site's most impassioned prose. Toph agreed to republish the essay under the condition that we append this message from him: "I believe Larkin Grimm."*

October 1, 2011. I'm sitting in the back of the Paramount Theatre in Asbury Park, watching Swans tear the place apart. It's not much to see. Excepting Thor Harris, the long haired auxiliary drummer stripped to his waist and striking poses appropriate to his Nordic deific namesake, they look almost genteel on stage. There are clues in the band's movements: leader Michael Gira's spastic gyrations; the hypnotic head lolling of bassist Christopher Pravdicha; the way Phil Puleo draws back his arms to hit his massive standing bass drum like he's pulling a sinking man out of quicksand, or about to bring the stake down into some demon's heart. But there's little visual complement to the guttural roar shaking the theatre. They just look like some older dudes in a rock band—some of them still too skinny, a couple aging well. They don't look like they could possibly be making the sound they are, which is like the amplifiers had been filled with their own blood, like they had taken that blood and slathered their strings with it. I've been in earthquakes with fewer undulations than this theater. I can barely comprehend it. But I do.

It seems to some like Swans are just mucking about on stage, but they're actually doing something that's crazy hard. Once you've been acquainted with rudiments of a few instruments, letting a single chord or note ring—and then, as Gira is wont to do at various moments, vibrating on stage like someone possessed, snake charmer and snake simultaneously—is not very difficult. Swans, however, have to pay strict attention to their surroundings and control these completely unstable chords. It's not merely that they're blessed with a calibrated sense of cosmic vibrations or whatever. The band often does not follow any meter, preferring visual cues rather than musical ones. It's as if Gira assembles a band meeting and concocts two hours worth of gestures and their associated fears. "When I wink my eye, we'll play D flat 6 add nine. The bell player will hit a gong. The pedal steel will channel the supernatural shrieks of children centuries dead from influenza." It's a master class in tensile showmanship, the mark of the highest professionalism, and it explains how after some decades the band can call this sound up at will. There's even a harmonica in the hollowed out crater of its one long, droning middle chord. That they then resolve this tension, such as they do, with a sinuous, resolutely anti-climactic tribal beat shows how finely tuned their counter-intuition is.

*****

Today I know the song to be "The Seer," the title track to 2012's best album. It's thirty-two minutes long and has, as its only lyric, the words "I see it all," repeated past the point of mantra, past the point of sense, where it ceases to be distinguishable at all from the "indecipherable obscenities" at the piece's conclusion. It's so massive it has a prologue in the home taped "The Wolf," a stalking harbinger that asks to be "splayed upon your silver gate" as a matter of pride. There's also "The Seer Returns," which, despite its relative funkiness, features the extremely unsettling wordless vocals of Jarboe while an interstellar answering machine describes, "a jagged, deep crack in the crust of the earth. Put your light in my mouth. Ahh the mountains are crumbling."

This is a 40-minute stretch that is easily the boldest move on 2 CDs (or 3 LPs) full of them. It begins with ghosts moaning on the helpfully titled "Lunacy," which features Low's Alan Sparhawk and Mimi Parker in a chorus that Brecht would certainly approve. They deliver the line "Your childhood ... is over" in such a shudder that one reaches past any musical contemporaries and starts flipping through The Tempest to find analogs. The album ends with ramblings about "a ladder to God! Ge ge ge ge ge a ladder to God!" that, in live renditions of this lyric's song, "The Apostate," Gira delivers as if on the verge of striking himself for each curse.

Suffice to say *The Seer* possesses a singular vision. It also represents a cumulative one: the metaphorical soul in the marble Gira has been hacking at for decades. Birthed in Manhattan's Lower East Side around the time of Sonic Youth and other no wave bands, Swans earned a reputation for making particularly nasty, brutal music even among their peers and competitors ("next to our friends the Swans, who had a percussionist who pounded metal, we were total wimps," Kim Gordon remembered of a 1982 tour). Over the ensuing decade-plus of lineup changes, Gira gradually sanded the barbs off his music without making it the least accessible. When keyboardist and vocalist Jarboe joined in 1985, the band's sound moved in a more overtly gothic, folk direction, which resulted in records, like 1996's supreme *Soundtracks For The Blind*, that may have been more hinged but no less violent. The record was elemental, as artsy as anything from New York but, to borrow a phrase from reviewer Greil Marcus, "as contrived as the weather."

The record would have a big influence on the post-rock bands of the coming decade, but Gira broke up the band, focusing on his creepy folk project Angels of Light. They reunited in 2010, abjuring almost all of their previously recorded music and roaring out of the gate with (2010). A sample song title from this album: "You Fucking People Make Me Sick." (I imagine Gira birthing this particularly bilious piece into the world, smiling, and saying to himself "the old uniform still fits.") In any iteration, Gira's interests lie in the thin tripwires between lunacy and divine inspiration—or perhaps smashing the differences, if there are to be had, between divine and demonic "touching." As Swans, he borrows the fortitude necessary to pick at the scabbing of these ideas—uses the blood and the pus of them, in fact, as his primary colors. *My Father*, the band's first in 16 years, is among their finest, and they followed it with a tour where they used the stage to dig even deeper. But not even this year's stunning live-album-slash-fundraiser *We Rose From Your Bed With The Sun In Our Head* could fully let on how deep The Seer would go.

*****

May 29, 2012. Three blocks from the ocean sits Monmouth Medical Center in Long Branch, NJ, and the view from my father's hospital window is astonishing. At 7 PM you can see the buildings' shadows grow long over Bath Ave. The daylight turns yellowish, the brick façade dulls. My father has a bandage on his chest where a tumor the size of a quarter used to be. He's sleeping under the influence of morphine, something he's never had use for but his son has experience abusing. 1% of North American breast cancer patients are men, and, as the joke goes in my family, my father has "won the booby prize." I chuckle along with my mother, wondering, silently, that jokes are great and all but why can't my old man just pull that tumor out with his teeth?

It will be months before I hear Karen Orzolek's gentle voice over the shapely acoustic waltz of "Song For A Warrior." To say it's the most beautiful song on the album and then walk away is irresponsible, and yet I don't know how to even mention it while doing it justice. There is something simultaneously comforting and terrifying, strange and yet understated, in the song that I've been unable to shake since August. I like Orzolek's other band, the Yeah Yeah Yeahs, just fine, but there's something about this performance, something about how audible her breath is. She sounds like a child at the beginning of a Kung Fu movie, narrating a Shogun's bloodlusty revenge in terms that are more elegiac and comforting than vengeful. This is no fight song, this is no reckoning, but it is instead a statement of support for the weight that the world's destroyer must bear. This is a matter-of-fact reading at the metaphysical weigh station. She seems to say that this is what must be done, and it may be impossible; and we love you.

The song always transports me to my father's hospital room. I'd like to think it owes more to the music—impossibly lugubrious even when utterly haunted, like the limpid late afternoon light on the day of his surgery. My father is no one's warrior—not even mine, as hard as he tried teaching me the finer points of stereo equalization and engine maintenance. If thereifixedit.com had been around when I was in grammar school, we would've run riot all over it. But the lyrics suggest some things about masculinity, something about fatherhood, and duty—all things that will forever, naturally, remind me of him—that I've been unable to parse, if not process. And I always lose it at the line where Orzolek says, "Some people say that God is long dead … but I heard something inside you with my head to your chest."

*****

My father believes in God, and I used to as well, but lately, I'm not too sure. I'm scared to death of admitting this to myself or others. So many of the 12-step meetings I attend talk about the Higher Power Which I Choose To Call God that it's become something of a secret shame. Mostly, they forget to even give the idea of "one's own conception of a higher power" any lip service whatsoever. "Solution-based meetings," they're called. "God is either nothing or he is everything. What was our choice to be?" they intone.

And when God is everything, he is EVERY thing: the hand that hides your keys when you're about to innocently drive to the neighborhood bar; the eyeglass case that obscures the phone when you're about to call your dealer; the five-dollar bill in your pocket on laundry day; the rambling drunk in the back of the clubhouse that manages to say something of substance the one day they attend these meetings. God has these people in the palm of His hand, and he accordingly acts as everything from an ambulance to a headhunter to a dayplanner to a post-it note. As for the tumor in your father's chest, the structures of your childhood washed away into the Atlantic ocean by Hurricane Sandy, the widows and orphans you see roaming the funeral parlors of your friends, well … God has a plan that's better than yours.

I'd be lying if I said I've never felt this way. This autumn, however, I'm mentally turning these church basements into the cover of a Cannibal Corpse album. My brain flashes images of scenes so violent, so sudden and sword-unsheathing sharp, that I even now hesitate to slow them down to write them here, in the comfort of my own bedroom. There are absolutely black, raging thoughts against other human beings that I don't remember ever having, not when there were all kinds of consciousness-blotting things coursing through my brain, not even after a previous break up where I literally set that woman's gifts and t-shirts on fire. This is God's plan? A life of crushing anxiety and ineptitude? A father with no chest? The Jersey Shore house still stood but the roller coaster was in the Atlantic. To the extent that I could see God's plan in any of this, it felt cruel. I felt like Michael Dawson being brought back to the island on *Lost*, only to keep a bomb from blowing up long enough to let Jin escape from the island. And now Christian Shepherd was standing before me, telling me, "You can go now, Christopher."

But if my embittered ranting is true, and God is nothing, and spirituality without religion is a sham, and life is some meaningless cipher, what is this thing, then? What is that heartbeat I remember feeling in my father's chest at the age of four, and why does that come back to me the nanosecond Karen O sings about it? If all of this is muscle and blood and sinews and gray brain matter and marking time til astral collisions, if all that my Father really is to me is a provider whose affections are borne from gross sentimentality, then what is that? Why does memory have the pull that it does? Why does this music speak to me in the way that it does? Why is the past year of my life and all of its petty, middle-class, white problems—stuck in the wrong job, pining for the wrong woman, eating the wrong food, trying to subside that pain in the wrong bedrooms—more bearable, even ecstatic, in the strains of music like this?

*****

There's a scene at the end of *Take Shelter* (2011) where we learn that Michael Shannon's apocalyptic dreams are real. Yellow, unctuous rain falls on his wife's hands, shaking in disbelief as dozens of funnel clouds burst from a previously serene day over the ocean. Her mind can't process it, but her senses are not lying to her. She knows what she's seeing is true, but she also knows that it can't be. But while her defense mechanisms are shaken, maybe irrevocably, she can handle her improbable but certain doom.

Swans make music that is aimed precisely for that moment, and the last moments of "Song For A Warrior" may be the band's finest execution. The music shifts to a dark, unstable chord at the end of the last verse, a choir joining behind Orzolek as she begs her warrior to "Send them home! Send them home! Use your sword, and your voice, and destroy…" Swans stay on this chord for far longer than they do on any other in the song—harmonically, in sequence, but atmospherically jarring as all hell, which is precisely what it sounds like, even as there are no usual mountains of dissonance or bells and percussion. It feels like the ground is going to rupture, you can practically see the red light shooting out of the cracks in the ground: "And destrooooooooooooooooooooooooy…"

But there the music hangs aloft. In *Take Shelter*, Michael Shannon takes his wife's oily hand in his. Throughout the film he has been an unbearable nervous wreck, almost certainly insane, never sure if every cloud or winged creature is the signal moment of the End. The worst of his fears are confirmed, yet now he is a source of strength for his wife and young daughter. I can see this scene in my mind's eye while "Song for a Warrior" ends at its pulchritudinous tonic chord, all whispers and tenderness: "Then, begin again." The couple walk into the house. The screen goes to black. The credits roll. The world ends. They die. So do we.

*****

October 28th 2012: Sandy makes landfall around 6 PM today, a

Monday. There were a lot of sights and sounds from that storm and its aftermath that I will never understand, whose visual or auditory evidence was literally unfathomable, but whose reality I must nevertheless accept. The size of the storm as it moved up the coast. The Seaside Heights roller coaster in the Atlantic Ocean. The picture of the yellow house in Union Beach that was half destroyed. Sea Bright and Sandy Hook underwater. Ocean Avenue on the ocean. How my neighbors' lights looked through my own powerless window for three nights as my mother and I sat staring at them through our window, dark and cold. The sound of elation when we got our power back after seven days. The sound of her voice when she told me she'd been sleeping at my friend's house all week.

But nothing was crazier than that Monday night into Tuesday morning, when the worst of the storm had passed but the wind gusts were still terrifying. There could not have been a working lightbulb within miles of Monmouth County. I was frightened and mind-boggled in a way I had never known (in fact I had joked to someone that I would never listen to Godspeed You! Black Emperor and Swans so blithely again—certainly not the Zorn-esque freak out of "93 Ave B Blues," which literally sounds like metal structures ripped apart). I was awake at 1 AM, reading by candlelight, when I noticed the house had gotten…brighter. I looked outside my window, and the clouds had parted just enough for the full moon to shine through. In the middle of the worst thing nature had ever thrown at me, among eviscerated trees, mass flooding, and suburban sprawl plunged into darkness: there was the motherfucking moon.

It vanished again moments later. The next light I'd see was my neighboring town's lights four days later.

*****

In 2012 I finally buckled down and finished *The Idiot* (1869). Dostoevsky was, famously, an Orthodox Christian, but his ideas of the divine nature of Christ and God are so far removed from even the judgmental, quarterly confessional Catholicism of my youth that I found it boggling. Dostoevsky suggested—or his characters did, anyway—that Christ had indeed died for our sins, but it had nothing to do with our salvation. Rather, Christ's death was to hold up this awful mirror to mankind and its socializing, cliquish, and duplicitous instincts. Prince Myshkin, the novel's stand-in for Christ (if not Dostoevsky, or both) is the victim of intense manipulations by a wealthy maniac, who, though he succeeds, only murders the prize he spends the entire novel coveting. Not only does the world think nothing of this turn of events, but Myshkin is the fool, openly mocked for cleaving so desperately to something—to ideals—that is killing him, because they cannot be traded for people or material or prestige.

The Idiot, like *The Seer*, like the antiseptic smell of hospitals and church basements, like power outages, like the ruins of the boardwalks of Asbury Park and Ocean Grove, like sleeping in an empty bed, will forever remind me of 2012. Finished 150 years apart, these two artworks posed the only questions worth asking in the year of our supposed apocalypse, questions beyond merely "why do bad things happen to good people?" "Why are bad things happening to me?" "Does anyone notice or care if I am kind to my neighbor?" Questions that are impossible to pose in any known language—it would sound something like, "why is it that when God is nothing I cannot stand the way I feel, and when God is everything I cannot the stand the way I act?"

Gira isn't so much bothered with the question of God's existence as he is fascinated by his seeming prophets. That would explain "The Apostate," the album's ultimate song and, at 23:01, only the second longest. It's another jam born out of the band's trademark primordial ooze of drone that evolves into the rantings of the divinely touched, deadly in both its earnestness and its irony. "It's not in my mind," shrieks Gira, convincing himself as much as the crowd of agape onlookers. "We're on an infinite line! Get out of my mind! Ge ge ge ge," he says, repeating the plosive like a Tommy Gun, like the repetitive nonsense was an incantation against the sick world, against unpleasant reality. "God, I can fly! WE'RE ON A LADDER TO GOD!" Perhaps it's coming out of the ground, from that jagged, deep crack spreading south to north. At least, until the ladder starts to fall apart: "Ge ge ge space cunt! Brain wash! Star dust! Space fuck! Cunt! Cunt!" he shouts, spastically. "We are blessed!" he screams, although the music is suggesting a different way to look at the same unwanted, supernatural presence. "We are blessed! Fuck! Bliss! Fuck! Bliss!"

If I had to summarize *The Seer*, I could say only that it's music that needs to be heard to be believed, and even then defying disbelief. It lives for disbelief, maps out the territory of the mind-boggle and then digs deeper, unraveling all of mankind if that's what it takes to for another addictive moment of transcendence, of unreality made manifest, of comfort irrevocably shattered and something new birthed, bloodily, into the psychic world. The seer sees what cannot be unseen, after all, and its maelstrom accepts no glad tidings. It forces upon us the one lesson the band learned in its earliest stages, the sound Gira has been chasing for thirty years, the one we can hear him shrieking in "The Apostate," as if he himself didn't want to learn it, much less admit it, much less be the voice for it. That the crazed are right: transcendence may, indeed, be real, but it is also fleeting, common, and, perhaps in the final analysis, unrewarding. We are blessed, indeed. Fuck bliss. Your childhood is over. I see it all. I see it all. I see it all. I see it all. I see it all.

THE "HAAOW, SWAY!?!?" AWARD FOR THEATRICALITY IN CRYBABYING

Eric Sams
17 December 2013

When Kanye West reeled back, tensed his muscles, and straight up lit into Sway Calloway midway through the pair's radio interview last month, it was like watching a python strike. I was mesmerized. I hadn't known what I was in for. All I knew about the clip was that 'Ye flipped out somewhere during his rambling, 34-minute "Sway in the Morning" interview. But "flip out" is not what he did. No, what Kanye did, in just the split-second it took him to scream "HAAOW, SWAY?!?!" into his mic, was give birth to a seething avatar of self-regard as wonderful and breathtaking as the inky monstrosity that clawed its way out of the fire priestess in *Game of Thrones*.

No man in modern history—maybe no man ever—has ever disappeared up his own asshole so totally, so quickly, and with such a wrathful vigor as Kanye did in that moment. "HAAOW, SWAY?I?I" Even as it hung there in the air between the two men it became his synecdoche. It wasn't shocking because he did it, it was shocking because he meant it. It was shocking because he was it. Does this seem harsh? If so, consider exactly what topic of discussion caused the eruption in the first place. To what meek suggestion came this rejoinder of pure id: "HAAOW, SWAY?!?!"

You probably already know that, by this point in the interview, Yeezy had already compared himself in one way or another to Steve Jobs, Shakespeare, Andy Warhol, Walt Disney, Leonardo DaVinci, and Will Ferrell's character from *Semi-Pro* (2008), so it's not surprising that his actual point got lost somewhere in there. His real goal in that interview was to shine a light on the injustice that kept him from being both the most famous hip-hop artist in the world and the most famous fashion designer in the world. Well, Sway asked, why couldn't he be? 'Ye began by positing that fashion executives were so blinded by his mic skills and production genius, they couldn't see that he was a fashion genius as well. As he went further, though, it became clear that he didn't buy that premise himself. That's when he started to make demands on the very fabric of spacetime. He bemoaned that every time he took a break from music to devote himself to fashion, people forgot that he Was (and Is, and Will Be) Yeezus, and they did wack ass things like put him on "the list" behind some wack motherfucker like Big Sean.

That's when it became apparent that Kanye didn't just want to be the ne plus ultra of the hip-hop and fashion worlds, he wanted to be able to rule over both of these domains at the same time and always. But, because being the best in the world at anything requires just…a stupid amount of work, and because staying the best may be even harder than being the best, it may very well be impossible to do it in two unrelated fields simultaneously. After all, even Yeezus can't collapse the temporal paradox that stops him from literally do two things at once.

Don't tell 'Ye that though, not if you want to keep that hand. Because a thing's being impossible in the abstract isn't nearly as important or meaningful as that thing being unobtainable for Kanye. And if he can't figure out how to do it, he sure as fuck isn't about to take advice from a dude in a knit stovepipe cap. "HAAOW, SWAY?!?!"

This attitude is the essence of Kanye. This attitude is also, of course, solipsism approaching clinical delusion, and to see it expressed so concretely, so forcefully, and so quickly was a true Christmas miracle. "HAAOW, SWAY?!?!?" It was like watching someone's leg jerk when the doctor hits their knee with his little rubber hammer. "HAAOW, SWAY?!?!"

This is the part where I was going to try to draw some parallel to my own life, and be all there's-a-little-Kanye-in-all-of-us. But that's not true. There isn't. Most of us can't fathom being flummoxed when faced with a literal impossibility, because, for us, keeping up with our e-mail is a task beyond reckoning. So when we use it as a catch phrase—and, to be clear, I'm going to be saying this a lot—we won't mean it like Kanye meant it. It's Kanye's world. Like, literally. You, me, and Sway just wouldn't understand.

A FEW THOUGHTS ON NIRVANA'S INDUCTION INTO THE ROCK AND ROLL HALL OF FAME

Conrad Amenta
13 April 2014

Nirvana made pop music, both in the sense that Kurt Cobain wrote songs that were structured and arranged in fairly traditional ways and played on traditional instruments, and in the sense that his music was very popular. So I won't presume to suggest that the band was credible in the sort of unimpeachable way we talk about emerging subcultural or underground trends being credible, or in the way we sometimes consider bands with an explicitly political agenda, like Pussy Riot, to be credible. On the surface of it—say, if you'd never heard Nirvana's music before, but you'd just read their Wikipedia entry—Nirvana seems like exactly the sort of band that should be a first-ballot Rock And Roll Hall of Fame inductee. They sold a lot of records. They're stylistically distinct. They distill a genre that influenced many other bands. They were important in the sense that they provide convenient shorthand to describe a particular period of rock's history.

But when you get to thinking about the sound of Nirvana—not the structure, and not the historical footnotes, but the animalistic, visceral, wounded howl of Kurt Cobain's voice and his stubborn refusal to say much of anything specifically—there's something about their induction that feels wrong. In a lot of ways, Cobain's lyrics predicted South Park morality: everything is stupid, and nothing, including what I'm doing right now, is exempt from mockery. There was a stubborn refusal to engage, a cynical, even nihilistic approach to living that negated concepts like politics and idealism.

Chuck Klosterman's recent essay on Kiss and that band's induction into the Hall got me to thinking about the Hall's function and the various problems associated (but perhaps not associated enough) with imbuing countercultural figures with institutional credibility. Klosterman argues that Kiss exemplifies the true face of rock music: not the myth of rock—which is to say, its idealized, romanticized self—but the venal, hedonistic, commercialized, compromised, misogynistic, stupid, sex-obsessed, addicted true face of rock music. Kiss are absolutely obnoxious, offensive, and very, very dumb, but they are self-consciously so, which is important, because they simultaneously embody and reflect rock's true values back at itself. To hate Kiss (as, I admit, I do) is to disclose that you hate a lot of what makes rock music rock music (which, again, I admit I do). Which is why Kiss had such a hard time getting into the Hall of Fame all of these years. For a rock institution to honor them would be to admit to less-than-flattering things about the genre it was established to honor.

Which leads me to believe that the Hall Of Fame's function is to maintain and enhance the mythology on which rock, or at least rock historians and critics, thrive: the notion of an individualistic, culturally relevant, politically engaged, meaningfully progressive, and aesthetically vibrant school of art. Rock can sometimes be some of those things; it's very rarely all of those things; most of the time it's none of those things. But instead of honoring those incredibly rare intersections of rock's mythological components by leaving them be, or perhaps honoring the change they made possible, the Hall cannot help but institutionalize by its very nature. It makes diverse elements relatable, common, and similar to one another, sacrificing the individual act, which may have approached some of those aspects of rock's idealized myth, at the altar of rock and roll itself. The Hall privileges the myth over the freedom to be different. It takes bands that are sometimes about something and makes them about nothing, except rock and roll. This isn't anything new—it's a tale as old as church frescos and gallery exhibitions. Curation destroys nuance.

Which is why Nirvana's surviving members could have done something truly significant and honorable by refusing to be inducted into the Rock and Roll Hall of Fame. As a band whose music was basically about how everything is stupid and life isn't worth living, Nirvana could have negated the importance of the Hall. Instead, the remaining members of Nirvana played some music with Joan Jett, a woman best known for her anthemic testimonial to a love of a thing whose routines she was enacting in the process of professing that love. Nirvana, like Jett, ate their own tail right there in front of everyone, and disappeared completely from relevance once and for all.

Watching Dave Grohl and Krist Novoselic on Jimmy Fallon recently, I was struck by how thoughtless the two sound in telling old Nirvana stories and what it means to enter the Hall Of Fame. Being in the band, and being in the Hall, are experiences that are, like everything else, just pretty cool, and to be accepted without question or ever leaving one's mark on the experience itself. Grohl and Novoselic have always seemed like affable guys, so it's no wonder their collective reaction to their initiation was to be stoked. But it's telling that another experience referenced in the interview was when they were asked by "Weird Al" Yankovic for permission to parody "Smells Like Teen Spirit." There's no order of values here; where once everything was stupid, now everything is acceptable. They chose to participate in that for no other reason than that a celebrity wanted them to, and in keeping with their underlying belief that nothing has meaning (even what is supposed to be their biggest and most culturally relevant song) they agreed. Grohl and Novoselic fail to see that their refusal to participate can imbue a seemingly worthless thing—one's independence—with some value.

I suspect that, at least near the end of his life, Cobain understood the value of not participating in a way that Grohl and Novoselic don't. We can imagine that Cobain's suicide was the ultimate act of opting out from the compromised conversation that rock enthusiasts, or at least those who wonder what rock music is supposed to be, have among themselves. We can imagine that his death was ultimately representative of a principle, poorly articulated but viscerally felt, in Nirvana's angry and profoundly alienated music.

Please understand here that I'm not trying to valorize or advocate for suicide, be it as an artistic statement or for personal reasons. What I'm trying to suggest is that if rock music—the institution or the individual—valued engagement with issues beyond its own mythology, then someone like Kurt Cobain may have felt they had more than a binary choice: to be a stupid, compromised rock star, or to refuse to participate. Cobain was left with an irreconcilable contradiction. He had an audience, but nothing meaningful to say to them, perhaps even because he had nothing meaningful to say. The rock myths on which he was weaned were totally bereft of nourishment. It's all right there in his suicide note: "All the warnings from the punk rock 101 courses over the years, since my first introduction to the, shall we say, ethics involved with independence and the embracement of your community has proven to be very true. I haven't felt the excitement of listening to as well as creating music along with reading and writing for too many years now. I feel guilty beyond words about these things."

That Nirvana is now inducted into the Rock and Roll Hall of Fame settles, for me, the argument that Kurt Cobain left unresolved when he committed suicide: whether or not this very popular band could have found a way to embody the countercultural, anti-institutional, punk rock ethos to which it aspired. In 2014, 20 years after Cobain's death, what could have been an occasion to interrogate the underlying mythologies that feed this commercial enterprise was instead an occasion for yet another series of glitzy events, token sympathy, and false connectedness. Instead we got two nice guys who don't seem to overthink anything, celebrating their final and total incorporation into the status quo. It seems like such harmless fun, which is to say, not like something that has any sort of burning platform or pressing agenda.

For those of us who grew up in the '90s and who now, in our mid-30s, look back at our teenage years and wonder what it all meant, we finally have our answer: nothing in particular.

IT'S JUST ROCK 'N' ROLL: THOUGHTS ON THE 20TH ANNIVERSARY OF DEFINITELY MAYBE

Maura McAndrew
22 April 2014

1994 was a busy year in rock 'n' roll—so much so that every time I go to the record store, there seems to be another "20th anniversary reissue" on the shelves. One of these records—Oasis's debut *Definitely Maybe* (1994)—is not garnering too much fanfare, at least stateside. This is likely attributable not to the album's place in popular history (it seems, especially in Britain, to be well-remembered and still beloved), but to the fact that it has already seen the release of a box set in 1996, followed by a DVD in 2004, and appears in countless unnecessary "best-of" polls of the type NME publishes monthly. Is another release really necessary? Liam Gallagher, who shared his characteristically Gallagher-esque feelings on Twitter, doesn't seem to think so: "HOW CAN YOU REMASTER SOMETHING THAT'S ALREADY MASTERED. DONT BUY INTO IT," he raged, adding the requisite "LET IT BE."

So in accordance with the younger, more belligerent Gallagher's wishes, I did not buy/will not buy the reissue. I did, however, just buy my first copy of *Definitely Maybe*, which was conveniently available in the used CD bin for about six bucks. I'm not sure why I never owned it before, besides the fact that I was too young and too American to know who Oasis was until "Wonderwall" hit, and by the time I was a full-fledged fan, I just somehow became familiar with the majority of *Definitely Maybe*. That's the thing about Oasis: they are the be-all end-all of commercial rock bands, and they'll make sure you hear their songs. No need to lift a finger.

Positioned as an antidote to the waning grunge influence of the time, *Definitely Maybe* is a supremely commercial record. In fact, it's so commercial that the band was successfully sued over the song "Shakermaker," whose melody was actually stolen from the Coca-Cola commercial jingle "I'd Like to Teach the World to Sing." Oasis is a band known for this sort of lack of nuance; they're a band whose art is predicated on the sense that nothing they say has any meaning whatsoever, except that it's vaguely recycled from the vast canon of rock 'n' roll (and, apparently, Coke commercials). And *Definitely Maybe* succeeds as a grunge antidote in the most obvious way possible: in its naked desire to be successful, to be beloved, to be immediately legendary, and to prove that simple is better, that you don't have to be a fucking student to connect with people through rock 'n' roll.

That label comes from one of my favorite belligerent Liam Gallagher quotes: in the wake of *OK Computer* (1997), he dubbed Radiohead "A boring bunch of fucking students," adding (presumably just to be colorful) "I'll kick their fuckin' heads in, man, because they're dicks." At the risk of being a "fucking student" about to get my head kicked in, allow me to over-analyze the ridiculous, trumped-up, gloriously intoxicating record that is *Definitely Maybe*. First of all, what makes *Definitely Maybe* by far the band's best record is the way it became a self-fulfilling prophecy through sheer ambition and bravado: it's a record about becoming the biggest rock stars on the planet, which they then did. Easy. It's noteworthy that it was about that process of becoming, not about being rock stars (like *What's the Story, Morning*

Glory? [1995]) or being tired of being rock stars (like *Be Here Now* [1997]) or being…y'know, dead inside (like all that stuff after *Be Here Now*).

But Oasis's instantaneous success is, of course, tied to the way they positioned themselves as products and promoters of the capital-"c" Canon of British rock music. This relates closely to a piece my fellow CMG staff writer Conrad Amenta wrote recently on Nirvana's induction into the Rock 'n' Roll Hall of Fame. He writes, "The Hall privileges the myth over the freedom to be different. It takes bands that are sometimes about something and makes them about nothing, except rock and roll." Nirvana is the wrong band for the Hall of Fame. Oasis, on the other hand, was made for it, as this statement about the Hall itself could just as easily be describing their point of view as a band. *Definitely Maybe* is, in its way, like a mini-tour of the Rock 'n' Roll Hall of Fame. It's a tour of the most popular points of rock 'n' roll history, tweaked just enough to convince us that it's rock's future. And we buy it, because it floods our ears with the most satisfying and comforting melodies possible, and it screams at us with walls of guitars, and it implores us to live forever.

Definitely Maybe is an album about nothing except rock music. But Oasis knows that. Not only is it purposely about nothing, the Gallagher brothers have made a point of consistently sneering in the face of anything that portends to be about anything. Radiohead makes an ideas album, and they're "fucking students." In the Gallaghers' world, those who sing about politics and the nitty-gritty of real life instead of champagne supernovas and the morning rain and trains and wanting to fly are met with the utmost disdain. "It's just rock 'n' roll," repeats *Definitely Maybe's* leadoff track ("Rock 'n' Roll Star"), and they mean it. And once that's established, Oasis is free to make the stupidest, catchiest, most album-y album they possible can.

Every song starts at 60 mph. Every chorus has a pre- and post-chorus. There's always a coda. The guitars are like jets taking off, Liam Gallagher turns words like "sunshine" into "sunsheeeeiiiiine." It's irresistible. It's a riot. And it's a great record.

Can you read Oasis's music, and *Definitely Maybe* in particular, as a pastiche of the lowest lows of Baby Boomer rock, with its ridiculous psychedelia and empty platitudes about individuality and love and changing the world? Absolutely. Are Noel and Liam Gallagher actually social critics, their work a commentary on that most self-important generation, the one whose premature nostalgia gave birth to the Rock 'n' Roll Hall of Fame? Hell no. And fuck off with that pussy schoolboy bullshit. Fucking students.

To conclude: Happy 20th anniversary, *Definitely Maybe*. It's a short period of time, really, for a band founded on the assumption that they would become overnight legends. I can't wait to see what they do for the 25th.

ALVVAYS: ALVVAYS

Corey Beasley
7 August 2014

Toronto, Ontario, Canada. City Hall. A secret room behind the mayor's office, accessible by pulling on a fake hardcover of Rush's Neil Peart's *The Masked Rider: Cycling In West Africa* (1996) hidden in the mayoral bookshelf. The hidden room is paneled exclusively in RICH, DARK OAK with LEATHER ACCENTS and PLUSH MAROON CARPETING. An enormous desk covered in GOLD LEAF takes up much of the space in the room. DRAKE, 27, a rapper, sits at the desk in an overstuffed chair with a big gold owl on top of it. He wears a purple bathrobe, basketball shorts, and several chains. He looks rather glum.

DRAKE: Bored, man. (From a bowl formerly containing Fruity Pebbles, he picks up a spoon made of solid gold. He stares at it, trying to bend it with his feelings. It does not yield.)

ROB FORD, 45, Mayor of Toronto, enters as the secret door spins. He wears a rumpled grey suit with a red power tie, both of which are soaked in his sweat. He glances around the room nervously, approaching the desk. In his hands he carries a silver platter, covered.

DRAKE: (sighs) Speak, Ford.

FORD: Mr. Mayor, sir, I have the city's latest cultural offerings for your approval.

DRAKE: Approach. (He beckons.)

(FORD uncovers platter, revealing books and CDs arranged atop a velvet pillow. He sets the platter on the desk and steps backward, standing at attention.)

DRAKE: Explain. (He shuffles through the items, tossing aside a manuscript by Margaret Atwood, a biography of Roy "Shrimp" Worters, and other assorted items.)

FORD: These Toronto-based cultural exports want the city's seal of approval, sir. You can review and either award them the official endorsement or not. Sir.

DRAKE: (Nodding, he pauses with a CD in hand, staring at its cover.) Identify this disc, Ford.

FORD: That's the debut album by Alvvays, sir. It's self-titled, I should mention. They're a rock band.

(DRAKE slides the CD into a compartment in his desk, and the opening riff of "Adult Diversion" plays on a state-of-the-art soundsystem. A simple kick-snare beat propels an interlocking riff from two nearly clean guitars, everything soaked in reverb. Molly Rankin's vocals dominate the mix, not as dead-eyed as Lana or Sky, but still decidedly disinterested—an appealing tool to carry her lovelorn, self-defacing lyrics.)

DRAKE: Hold up. (He rewinds the track to catch a lyric.) "How do I get close to you / Even if you don't notice / As I admire you on the subway?" (He clicks play and croons the line over the song.) That's real, right there. Ford, you ever see the most beautiful woman in the world on the subway with you, and you know she'll be gone forever in just a few seconds? (Hangs his head.) Damn.

FORD: Our subway system covers 42.4 miles. Haha! (Smiles and fidgets.)

DRAKE: "One more cocktail / And I'm on your trail." Love how resigned she sounds there. Like, she knows that's just how it goes. (Scribbles this last rhyme on a notepad for later use.) And the way the guitar hook in the chorus mimics her vocal melody? Straight simple, but I'm like—yeah.

FORD: A fun tune to be sure, sir.

DRAKE: "Tune." Corny.

FORD: (Sweats.)

("Archie, Marry Me" kicks in, Rankin's vocals swooning above jangling guitars. Her dry wit and SAT-approved lyrics—"You've expressed explicitly your contempt for matrimony / You've student loans to pay and will not risk the alimony"—stay comfortably on the side of Camera Obscura cleverness rather than toeing into Decemberists preciousness. Any band that can go toe to toe with Camera Obscura, even for just one song, deserves more attention that a stage direction can give. Alas.)

DRAKE: This is the hit, isn't it?

FORD: (Checking his notes) This is the single, yes, your mayoralness, sir. Do you approve?

(The chorus hits, Rankin making her proposal—"Hey, hey! / Marry me, Archie!"—in a flash of understated, sheer pop bliss, a chorus so immediate you're sure you've heard it before, years back on "120 Minutes" or your college radio station. The melody sticks to the walls of the room, refuses to leave.)

DRAKE: Archie's lucky, man. What's he got I don't? (Flips through a stack of hundreds. When this doesn't cheer him, he reaches beneath his desk to grab two handfuls of silver dollars from a bucket. DRAKE tosses the silver dollars over his head and lets them fall in a shower of currency.)

FORD: Sir, if I may—don't get discouraged. It's the music you're evaluating, after all.

DRAKE: I said I liked it, didn't I? (Smashes fist onto desk) What else does this sound like, anyway? You know 40 doesn't let me listen to shit like this.

FORD: He worries about your palpitations, sir.

DRAKE: Just me, myself, and all my cardiac illness.

FORD: Don't worry. We don't have to talk to 40. I can find someone else. Just hold on, sir. (He presses a buzzer on the wall and talks through an intercom.) Deborah? Find me a youth.

(A few moments later, a YOUTH, clad in a barista's apron, with geometric tattoos on one arm and a scar where a lip ring had been, stumbles into the room. He wears a blindfold.)

YOUTH: Where am I? What's going on?

FORD: (Reddens, spittle flying from his mouth. Yelling.) CALM YOURSELF. You're here to help your CITY, you vapid SHITWIT.

DRAKE: Easy, man, easy.

YOUTH: Who's that? I recognize that voice.

FORD: QUIET. Listen to this music. (He plays a few tracks, "The Agency Group," "Ones Who Love You," and "Dives". The YOUTH listens, shuffling from one foot to another. He seems vaguely frightened, but the music calms him.) Now, what other rock'n'roll bands do these tunes resemble?

YOUTH: "Tunes." Corny. I don't know, man—it's good, but it sounds like every other guitar-pop band with a synth or a drum machine out there right now. It doesn't not sound like Real Estate or DIIV or Smith Westerns or any of that stuff. But see, I hate those bands. Cheesy, easy-breezy bullshit. Somehow, this is ... better. Way better. Maybe it's the chick's voice? Something about how her vocals elevate the music behind it, which is all fairly simple, lots of high-necked melodies. Basic structures, verse-chorus-verse, bridge where the music drops out for a few measures, chorus. If it ain't broke, et cetera.

FORD: All right, that's enough. Back to your Cultural Studies program. (He pushes the YOUTH through the spinning secret door.)

YOUTH: How'd you know—(Exits.)

DRAKE: Was dude saying shit sounds like everything else out there? I can't put the Toronto stamp on that shit if it isn't pure gold, you feel?

FORD: No, of course, I understand. But—

(A knock on the door. FORD and DRAKE share a confused look. The door spins open, and GEDDY LEE, 60, musician, walks into the room. His hair has been recently conditioned.)

LEE: What's shaking, fellow Torontonians? My sixth sense told me you were discussing prodigal talent in musicianship. I'm just stopping by to tell you—hey! Not everyone can be a Neil Peart. If you're writing solid songs, you don't have to be the best drummer or bassist or singer in the world. Pop music is hard! Reinventing pop music is even harder. So, if it hooks you, enjoy it. That's my advice. Take care, now! (Laughs heartily, and exits.)

DRAKE: Man's got a point.

FORD: You're feeling better about the album, then, sir? Do you want to give Alvvays Toronto's full approval?

DRAKE: I'm almost there. I'm waiting for one more push, one song you just can't argue with, you know? Unfuckwithable. Also, Ford, I'm hungry.

(At the sound of that last word, ABEL TESFAYE, 24, musician, enters. He bends at the waist and averts his eyes from DRAKE, staying in this posture as he walks to the desk to deliver a Rueben. He dares not speak. Sandwich delivered, he withdraws into the darkness. DRAKE chews.)

FORD: I think I have just what you ordered. (He plays "Party Police," a perfect piece of downcast power-pop, its adolescent longing achingly communicated through Rankin's best vocal performance on the record, matched with her most intuitive hooks. "You don't have to leave," she sings, "You could just stay here with me / Forget all the party police," the chorus's melody an inch shy of monotone and heartbreaking in its simplicity.)

DRAKE: Party police. Damn—I know those types, always watching you with your girl, ready to snitch or sell your picture to the paparazzi if y'all go upstairs or leave together. Keeping people from being happy. Jealous, man, always so jealous of what you got. And if you let them dictate? They win, and you go home alone. Shit's real.

FORD: I thought you'd approve, sir. It's the best pop song I've heard in ages. (He smiles, clearly pleased with himself.)

(CARLOS DELGADO, 42, baseball player, enters, wearing a Toronto Blue Jays jersey and carrying a baseball bat. FORD bows to him, shocked.)

DELGADO: Let me tell you, boys, and I should know—that track is a home run. (He swings the bat in a perfect arc, looking out into the middle distance at an imaginary grand slam. He tips his cap and leaves.)

DRAKE: This is going on for too long, isn't it?

FORD: Absolutely. Should we wrap it up?

DRAKE: Yeah. Alvvays gets the Toronto stamp. Makes me proud of that north north, that up top.

FORD: (lights and smokes 20 cigarettes at once)

DRAKE: I hate this job.

TIME WASHES EVERYTHING AWAY:
A DIRTY BEACHES
RETROSPECTIVE

Robin Smith
14 November 2014

There are places where trains run twenty-four hours a day, where that thing we call the end of the line doesn't really exist—though the connections to places beyond do. There are stops where warm, automated voices say "change here" and mean it as a prediction, not a suggestion. There are journeys that start in one direction and then go in another, where passengers sit in silence in cities they're not from. There's a lot of swapping and beginning to belong and ceasing to settle down, and it all happens because of wheels and routes. There are drifters. They get on and get off and get on.

Alex Hungtai is a drifter. There's only so much cash in his wallet, only so many conversations he can have with the same people, only so many streets he can walk down before he's looked up at every building. Since he's been a musician, it seems he's always been writing about displacement—or else writing with it. On *Badlands* (2011) it was tucked away in his pocket, his lo-fi crooner ballads coloured with the unease that now slithers through his music. Riffs were stolen from faraway noise bands and highways were celebrated; a sense of rock's freewheeling potentiality was caged away in his mind. He longed for wind through his hair but was conjuring the images from a bedroom where he could only reproduce the sensation.

It never came, but *Drifters* (2013) did: a heart-breaking, artificed journey through the night that captured Hungtai at his most hopelessly nomadic—getting on to leave and getting off to scream at every new destination. The songs sounded like they were running through houseless cities, full of buildings with bright, glitzy billboards and empty rooms. Inspired by Suicide's forward-motion synth-punk, they rolled onward, the tracks clunking awkwardly under Hungtai's determined feet. Unlike Suicide, he couldn't find one thing worth laughing about—his screams were inflected with tragic sighs and measured fist pumps, like a wolf howling at the moon on a moving trolley.

In Hungtai's music, two things are forever: transience and despair. His songs are tied to both, and tend to watch them coincide, knowing that one is shadowed by the other. *Drifters* was presented with *Love is the Devil* (2013), an uncomfortable ambient record that was about as warming as sepia toned pictures of strangers, taken a hundred years ago. The record's sharp strings and unmodulated, droning fogginess made for a history lesson of Hungtai's romantic tragedies and personal failures, but it didn't feel like it was finished. Listening to it now, the pain doesn't feel any further away; its archaic production and far-removed classical resonations speak to a constant, renewed suffering, serving as living proof that the oldest traditions can be married to a brand new heartbreak. That's one thing a journey through the night can't take away.

Hungtai recently said that "all pain is temporary," but it's the one emotion that's endured through all his work. It's Dirty Beaches' only consistent aesthetic. His new and final record, *Stateless* (2014), is wounded by leaving, in a very permanent way. Within the worlds of his earlier work, pain only felt temporary, because there was promise of the next place to fuck up: on *Badlands*, his half-smiled pop songs suggested that this would soon be the past. Grooves were never crushed, but instead faded away, suggesting the intangible kind of division that takes place the further down the motorway you are. On *Drifters*, though, Hungtai realised that going away and staying put are two actions performed at once. You can re-emerge in a different place, and be changed because of it, but zip codes are phases, part of a numerical system you pass through.

On Stateless, there are no rhythms to be carried by, no beats provoking movement, and, crucially, Hungtai isn't singing. His vocals had radically different persuasions on *Badlands* and *Drifters*, but they were a reminder of mortality and its role in displacing individuals. Stateless is different, though. This place neglects Hungtai, but with its constant hum and never-ending bluster, its focus turns to the next drifter. Pain is temporary for one, but not for all. It's similar to Love is the Devil in this way, because it suggests a sickness that lives on long after your band or your body is gone—a sickness contracted to others in photos, buildings, and textbooks.

When he wrote *Love is the Devil*, Hungtai described himself as a "rotten piece of shit," but introducing this record, he talks in the first person plural—these are "our" mistakes, "our" nothing. There are no melodies in Stateless, so the city doesn't feel personal; it doesn't crease into Hungtai's exit routes. Outside of the music, his destination is clearer, but inside there's no analysis of this as Dirty Beaches' final chapter. There's no singing, so he doesn't say goodbye. Instead, he gets trapped within methods and "algorithms," things that will process others after him.

Parting the synth-laden ambience are a droning saxophone, that whistles like wind, and a slow-moving viola that struggles around skyscrapers. It suggests movement the way it happens in a bad dream where you want to run away but can only run in place. For Hungtai, it's the ultimate nightmare: no more drifting. Him and collaborator Vittorio Demarin are credited for the music on Stateless, but it's more likely they've been trapped inside it. The music swallows them. The meditative ambience that comprises the record's four pieces make it noisier and more difficult than the most dissonant of experiments—the layers on "Pacific Ocean," in particular, busy one another like architecture peaking out behind more architecture. For the last Dirty Beaches record, that feels fitting: *Stateless* loses Hungtai, who has always dreamt of his next turnover, within the city itself, among its bizarrely folded infrastructure. All that remains are the buildings on the front cover of the record, which look entirely fake—like they've been rendered, rather than photographed.

So when I listen to *Stateless*, I don't see Hungtai. He's not in the picture like he is in the strangely blissful covers for Badlands and Drifters—Dirty Beaches already lost its protagonist with Love is the Devil. But I am reminded of an earlier version of him that I briefly saw, one night last year: that night, I saw Hungtai play at Leeds' Brudenell Social Club, a gig that was disastrously promoted but understandably obscure. At the last minute, the venue billed Hungtai as additional support for post-hardcore kids Rolo Tomassi. The damage didn't seem enormous at the time, but it was. Instead of playing to a room empty but for the shrugging shoulders in the corners, he played to a few eye-rollers testing out their appetite for punk. It's not their fault, but the atmosphere became furious. The bemused sniggers were counterpointed by Hungtai throwing his mic stand into the empty space in front of the stage, like a tool he'd been cheaply compensated with after hours of wasted work. Every chest pump felt more unwilling, every scream more reasoned by the mistreatment. The place bore down on Hungtai, isolating and extracting him, deciding upon his very movements. And then he was done.

I wanted him to say something about it after the show, but he didn't. He thanked the audience and moved on. I wanted him to spread the word online, but there were only more of his positive retweets, the ones that are replenished every day, even now, in the dozens. And then he went to the next city, probably London, the city of all cities, where something else happened—maybe you can fill me in on that. All I know is that he was touring, drifting, living miles and miles from the memory he had just created for me: one of the most inspiring and terrifying nights of my life. It might have meant nothing to him, and as the wheels spun over the asphalt, the night might have truly been washed away. But if I could capture that show—in a picture, in a drone—it would last forever. Time can make you forget, but memories wash up on new shores.

INTERLUDE:
THE COKEMACHINEGLOW INDEX

7557 total articles, including current and deleted blurbs and blog posts, etc.

103 interviews

207 podcasts total

8 fantasy covers podcasts, in which CMG favorite artists covered songs by other CMG favorite artists

1157 track reviews

3345 record reviews

170 "articles," or open-ended pieces before we started a blog to house them

94 festival features

142 concert reviews

198 year-end awards

13 year-end lists

3 Halfstravaganzas, a.k.a mid-year celebrations of, um, the previous six months of music

2 Listravaganzas, in which we did every list we could think of

3 Hatebags, which collected our most recent batch of reader hate mail (this was before Twitter)

78 writers total if we go back to 2002, not including fake authors like Zach Braff's Beak, Edgar White, and that Tom Waits advice column, etc.

4 articles including the word "butterfuck"

1 mentioning Laura Dern

338 No Big Hair posts

46 counterpoints

MOUNT EERIE: SAUNA

Adam Downer
26 February 2015

The first thing you'll notice about *Sauna* (2015) is the setting. Phil Elverum opens what is otherwise the coldest album of the young year by blowing on an ember. Soon a fire comes to life, with wood crackling beneath a warm synth chord that ever so slowly builds to insufferable heat. Several quiet minutes of timbre fluctuations pass before Elverum begins singing a fluttering melody to himself. The words are almost background noise, a babble muttered as if it didn't care if it was heard or not, until he calls the song into being with a freezing couplet: "I don't think the world still exists. Only this room in snow."

The log cabin is a cliché setting for emotional detox, the place the artist goes in order to exorcise some demon, usually an ex-lover (see: *For Emma, Forever Ago* [2007]). Sauna isn't so romantic. Its cabin sits in the middle of a frozen wasteland independent from the rhythmic pulse of time, its demon the fraying knot tying existence and purpose together. "Emptiness" is a tangible character on Sauna, a nebulous enemy not unlike *The NeverEnding Story*'s (1979) The Nothing. It fills everything with the same sort of massive sorrow. Bags, pumpkins, and Elverum himself are not described as having "nothing" in them, but rather Emptiness. For *Sauna*, Emptiness is a massive muffler. *Sauna* is a folk, rock, and indie record struggling to be heard over impenetrable drones. The moments Elverum cracks through are characterized by an icy hopelessness, full of weighted, stark observations like "I can't remember when (or if) I woke up," "A tractor idling two blocks away in the fog, unseen," "I walked to the bookstore in a rain that silently filled the air." Before the songs themselves start to really register, the thing you'll notice about *Sauna* is how heavy the whole thing is.

Underneath this isolating exterior is a stormy record with dashes of menace. *Sauna* simmers with a bitterness that doesn't come out in poetic bile but rather in Elverum's quiet, assured vocals and in the record's musky makeup. In the opening three tracks, wind, guitars, drums, and Elverum compete for your ear's attention until they form a gorgeous clutter. Vocals paint a lonely existence of wandering around, confused—"Dragon" ends with the grammatically stilted "Going into the basement again, I reach down beneath the human." There are hints of darkness, dissonances held a bit long, references to a "dragon that roars" dropped quietly. The dragon doesn't show until the overwhelming, dissonant synth chord kicking off "Emptiness" and *Sauna*'s angrier, musically heavy middle section. After *Sauna* opened with sad coldness, the massive tonal shift turns it almost frantic. In "Boat," Elverum muses "I was born from nowhere, and to nowhere I'll return," as if he were totally unaware of the earthquake of drums bashing underneath him or the guitars tremolo-picked into a tidal wave. Next to the storm he creates, he stays hushed, letting his timid voice be supplemented by the great cacophony that's communicating more about the music's character than his voice and lyrics could do alone.

That character is cold and deep but there's something alluring about it nonetheless. It is not that there's a secret heart of optimism peeking through *Sauna*. It's that there isn't one. *Sauna* offers a glimpse of depression settling over the world like a veil, and sounds the terror of living underneath. From here, Elverum communicates a melancholy confusion, his environment falling apart—the basement is flooded, he's trapped in his boat at sea, the metaphors piling on top of one another as Elverum works to explain the extent of isolation. In "Spring," hellish organ chords call and hellish choir chords respond, the two of them trudging through a landscape of feedback and drone. Towards the end, the elements subside, leaving Elverum, locked in tight harmony, frantically delivering lyrics like a prayer. It's the most inhuman *Sauna* gets, a climax channeling the other side, hell sprung into existence. It's the darkness simmering beneath Sauna brought to life.

Sauna is not fun to listen to, but it is very powerful. It's an "unconventionally" pretty record, memorable for how effective it is at creating a tone so singularly dark without ever playing to sentimentality, how it is so filled with Emptiness but hardly catatonic. It seethes and sizzles and leaves a powerful tension in its wake. "Youth," the final track, ends with a methodical beat, nothing changed, no catharsis reached. But in the listener, there remains a sense of lived experience, a trip to that precipice between reality and Emptiness. *Sauna* goes to a scary place, so there's relief when it ends. There is also, however, a very strong impulse to go back.

THE BALLAD OF SWAN LAKE

Brent Ables
17 November 2015

I thought I was on the inside…

I recently saw Moonface for the first time at a sandwich shop in Ottawa. We can count it that way if you don't identify Moonface with Spencer Krug. I don't. Him, Krug, I've seen, and thought I've known. I've maintained over the last decade the kind of relationship with his music—and that of his British Columbian compatriots, Daniel Bejar and Carey Mercer—that, being grounded in a lack of actual connection, is all retrojection and echo. It's sustained me more than anything else not subject to gravity.

But Moonface is not Spencer Krug. It's a mask, maybe even a mask covering a mask, a simulacrum whose own mask is mutability, a mask unmade and remade at will. I don't know if Krug is the phoenix yet—he has officially ditched the piano, if you're keeping track—but it was hot in that sandwich shop. I may have even sweated more than him. But I stood up front anyway, wearing my hat a bit looser now, trying to want it enough. Did I learn any secrets? They were in the music, which was fantastic. But the music wasn't there, with the bodies changing in time. Before the end I went where it was cooler: outside.

…But now I know it's still a secret…

Q: "Are there any trends that you find frustrating or disappointing? Are there any trends in music today that you find exciting or inspiring?"

Krug: "My initial answer to this question was a long rant about how excited I was to see online music journalism starting to wane. I thought maybe some of the hundreds of blogs were starting to lose some of their dubious credibility … It's often frustrating to see how music is written about on the internet. There are many nonsensical similes and metaphors that say nothing in particular. There is a lot of writing that is more a showing off of vocabulary than a comprehensible description of what something sounds like; writing that's more an attempt to make the reader notice the writer, rather than the music … Also, there is often the building up of new acts in an attempt to appear cutting-edge, and then the tearing down of these same acts a year or two later, in an attempt, again, to appear cutting-edge. And in this way, there is a total lack of accountability. Also in this way, there is the championing of originality, but only that originality which falls safely within the parameters set and determined by whichever hundred voices are chattering at the time, agreeing with one another. This demands that artists walk a middle line; be something that can be comfortably yet hiply endorsed, even implicitly discovered, but then later shat upon, safely, if it will make the website look discerning. But this is 'demanded' of an artist only if he / she / they are seeking the approval of the online critics. If they are not, then it becomes remarkably easy to be only slightly annoyed now and then, and the rest of the time just say fuck all y'all.

"I know I must sound bitter, but I'm not, not really, not any more than any other musician I've talked with on this subject. So much online writing just seems totally irresponsible, and it's weird that it's still allowed to happen … What I'm complaining about here affects (and annoys) musicians and readers everywhere. It's a specific, half-assed, petty type of journalism found online that's just getting so fucking OLD—across the board. So basically, come on internet—try harder.[1]"

…The three of us together forever in debt…

Pickpocket's Locket (2015) and *Poison Season* (2015) were both released on August 28, the day after that Moonface show. Though I like to entertain myself with thoughts of arcane pacts between Swan Lake alumni, this shared release date is likely a coincidence. These records also mark the first time both artists have significantly integrated string arrangements into their music, MIDI and *Your Blues* (2004) notwithstanding. The "co-" doesn't belong in this incidence either, but perhaps it's not exactly an accident. ("Oh, you're putting violins on your song? That's a cool idea, lemme text Krug.")

Beyond these superficial links, at the level of content, the records have admittedly little in common. If there was ever much cross-musical influence between these two projects—and I would argue that even when they were regularly appearing on the same records circa 2005-2008, there really wasn't—they have certainly gone on their own paths now. Beyond friendship, whatever binds Bejar and Mercer together in 2015 lies at some other, rarified level. Whiskey and health commutes; darkness and the sublime. Canada.

I'm not going to review these records. To me, these are not artifacts made by animals, or commodities made for consumers, or expressions of the emotions of human beings. They are commandments, writ in stone, and whether I even really like them or not, I live by

[1]   http://wolfparade.nonstuff.com/5-questions-with-spencer/

them. These traces of gods whose names resound with mythopoeic force: KRUG. And did you know "Bejar," or its etymological ancestor, originally meant "place of the beehives?" That's a factum straight out of Edward Gibbon's classic banger, *History Of The Decline And Fall Of The Roman Empire* (1776). Bejar probably has a dog-eared copy of this volume on the upstairs toilet. But I learned it on Wikipedia, through Google—these are the names of our decline, and our fall.

…I sat down and took a number at the table where death resides…

I am old enough to find myself keenly interested in how these three men age. That might sound callous or superficial; I don't mean it that way. (As my girlfriend reported after the Ottawa show, Krug in particular has aged quite beautifully.) They age on record; they exist, in time, from song to song, right before our ears. But they do it differently, singularly in each case, and this is what fascinates me. Death is at once what is most universal and most personal to all of us; the more we acknowledge its inevitability, the less we accept its reality. This is why we need art that reaches into that darkness—so that we can greet it, when it comes, as a friend.

Carey Mercer's own encounters with mortality and its limits have been quite openly documented over the course of his last two albums. Though Mercer himself has been the source of all this information, the way it was discussed in the music press has always made me deeply uncomfortable; I consciously avoided the topic altogether when I attempted to pay tribute to Carey's *Cold Spring*, Cokemachineglow's #1 album of 2013 and the last to ever receive that honor. In his work with Frog Eyes, Mercer talks about himself, and even names records after himself, but he doesn't often sing about himself. He sings about traitors, addicts, generals, daughters, harpies, donkeys; war, plague, famine, poverty, heartbreak, uplift; transgression, transcendence, transascendence.

Dan Bejar, on the surface, doesn't seem much concerned with death. He's the eternal beatnik, eyes and mind on the horizon, with all the proper names it promises. Though Krug has done an admirable amount of exploration under the elastic Moonface moniker, Bejar has always been the truly Protean figure in this crowd. He's gone from the lo-est of fis to immaculate chamber pop to pub rock to soft-dick rock to, most recently, a kind of nihilist schmaltz that hits the halfway point between Sinatra and "Myrrhman." Of course, this continuous variation may itself be a kind of flight from death, insofar as it is a formal affirmation of the nature of life itself. But because Bejar never raises this vitality to the level of a theme, I have never felt that, even at its best, his work has the same depth of impact as that of his peers.

Which leaves Spencer Krug. Way back in 2009, Krug gave us indie rock's greatest extended reflection on aging with the opening triptych of *Dragonslayer*. "Silver Moons" sets the stage with a kind of melancholy self-send-off: "Maybe these days are over, over now / And I loved them better than anyone else, you know / But I believe in growing old with grace…" Naturally, the theme is explored through Krug's characteristic flame-language: "Gone are the days bonfires made me think of you / Looks like the prophecy came true / You are a falling tree, I am a falling tree / How old are you?—no, how old are you?" But just as things seem ready to wind down, or settle down, we get the palm-muted rawk of "Idiot Heart." Here we learn that you can't, can't settle down until you've raged, raged against the dying of the light … a bit. The song's placement between "Silver Moons" and "Apollo And The Buffalo…" clearly marks it as an escape, a line of flight, and its drama marks it as a performative affirmation of the very resilience to decay it speaks of. For my part, though, I never found the song very danceable.

This takes us to "Apollo And The Buffalo And Anna Anna Anna Oh!", which is almost certainly the best song ever recorded by Sunset Rubdown. The track begins abstractly, with some of Krug's most esoteric and evocative imagery: "The buffalo had given up on the world / And Apollo, Apollo is kissing all the valley girls / We climbed up the cross on the mountain on New Year's Eve / It was just God, the blizzard, the dreamweaver, and me." And then, out of nowhere, right at the gut: "But my God, I miss the way it used to be." Anna in this song is deliberately presented more as a symbol than a person, as if to emphasize that when our friends and lovers grow old and apart, all we have left to apply to the fading emotions are shifting names whose sense becomes increasingly irrelevant with time and distance. By the end, Anna's adoption of a new, unknown name has become a metaphor for the passage of time and the death instinct it portends.

Krug has sometimes been criticized for taking an overly intellectual approach to his music, as if it were more calculation than inspiration, and there may be some truth to this. But at its best, the complicated lyrical and compositional machinery of his massive songs works only to disclose a deep, entirely open emotional wound that would have no significance if approached directly. Just as a great novel will never open with its deepest insight or greatest tragedy, we shouldn't expect musical catharsis to come easy. Krug understands this so well that when the moments of release do come, they're both inevitable and cripplingly powerful. And his music hasn't lost this power in the intervening years, despite Krug's shift towards a less feral, more domestic aesthetic. Anyone who doubts this should go back and listen to "Daughter Of A Dove" from last year's *City Wrecker* EP, which contains one of the most astonishing crescendoes in recent musical memory. The song doesn't say anything profound about death, or God, or mortality. It's not a conduit to divine truth, or infernal wisdom. It doesn't say much of anything, really. But it exists, and it transports me completely, and that is exactly as spiritual as I need it to be.

…Borrowed an ascot to cover my eyes from the flame that awaited…

We aren't where postmodernism was supposed to leave us. The message got mixed somewhere: instead of leading us to the ground so that we could tear it up, semiology took on a life of its own, and we forgot to forget the simulacrum isn't actually real. Thus was born a society that lives entirely on the surface. Hierarchy being abolished, only a binary decision remained: balance yourself on the surface, present yourself as a surface, or fall off the edge of the new, two-dimensional earth. But on a surface, points are distinguished only by location, and above all not through the relative displacement of evaluation. Thus was born a historically unprecedented critical ethos: Everybody likes everything.

I'm not myopic enough not to understand that there are very good sociopolitical reasons for the unconditional affirmation of diversity in art. But of course, affirmation is never unconditional; there's always an Other, even when the Other is brought home. And so we end up in the odd situation that the least acceptable thing for a critic to do is present reasons for liking or not liking an artwork that have nothing to do with the identity of the artist in question. Nor does this apply only to critics; on the contrary, when *Pitchfork* interviewed Bejar prior to the release of *Poison Season*, it was Bejar who found himself in the awkward position of questioning whether Taylor Swift's music really deserves the attention and adulation it's gotten from the same people who, a generation ago, eschewed Madonna for the Pixies. I'm not interested in ragging on *Pitchfork*—they've done more than other entity on earth, including us, to promote the careers of these guys—but it's hard not to cringe at the interviewer's blithe response to Bejar's speech: "Do you ever worry about being out-of-touch?"

Far be it from me to put Bejar or anyone else in the position of spokesman for something they'd rather avoid talking about altogether, but: bless the out-of-touch. There is entirely too much touching today. We're all packed into the same small venue called the internet, the stage is a mirror, the mirror is a body, and the body is ours—can we not still empty it of organs? The body wants to be its own; why put the body where the body don't wanna go?

If we trace a spherical surface to its genesis, all points converge in a singularity. The center of the earth is the center for everyone. This is the only danger of unchecked disjunctive affirmation: we forget that we are all human beings, whatever else we might be. Our fires burn at different intensities—but at death, as our souls rise like burning shades of light, is it not the same point to which we ascend? We need art that gives that light shape, and lets it speak for all of us at once, in the same voice. In Mercer's shrieking guitars, Krug's baroque epiphanies, and the bittersweet paradoxes of Bejar's finest koans, I feel something slip from beneath the surface that I want to believe every person can feel, and should have the chance to feel. But I no longer have any idea whether this is my own ground rising to the surface, or me sinking into the depths, and the light fades either way.

…Now these beautiful days just seem dated…

I don't really go to shows much anymore. My brief, weird tenure as an online music critic is over at the end of the year. I've listened to maybe 20 albums this year, and liked about seven of them. The quality of my speakers? Poor.

But still, I'm glad I made that Moonface show at that sandwich shop in Ottawa. It was not particularly memorable for what it was—certainly not as memorable as Wolf Parade in 2005, or Sunset Rubdown in 2007. But I think maybe those days are over, over now. Memory has a way of closing up as you get older, so you have to select what matters and keep it close. If I remember this concert in a year, it likely won't be for the songs that were played, or the length of Krug's hair (long!), or even the fact that I managed to drag along my girlfriend's entire family, thus contributing more substantially to the man's career than I probably have ever done with all these thousands of stupid words on the internet.

What I will remember was just how excited Spencer Krug seemed to be playing music to the 40 or so people in that small, hot room. Because if there's still music left for him to create, and me to love, then neither of us are entirely spent. And if this means only, minimally, that our mutual self-spending can continue a little longer, then one can learn to take this as enough. All fires have to burn.

Alive.

To live.

…and fine.

JAMIE XX: IN COLOUR

Chet Betz
Published as part of CMG's final year-end roundup, in 2015

Music is a blessing. That's pretty much been the simple sum of my whole critical aim, saying that. I say it over and over again. I say it in mildly different manners, sure, but if you've read any of my stuff here or elsewhere then you've read plenty of Betz doing Betz. If I'm not talking about rap then you can tell when I really love something because I find a way to start talking about Tarkovsky or Cronenberg. I'm obsessed with Boethius's concept of the eternal moment; I also pretend that everyone else had the same Intro to Philosophy class that I did in college. "Music of the spheres"—into it, big time, I'm an absolute ideal-chaser if ever there was one. And Keats' whole thing about truth is beauty and beauty truth? Yeah, that's my steez. I get on that Bible tip, too, Old Testament-style, in case you find your music reviews wanting for mentions of Eden and capital-F floods and, my favorite: living sacrifice.

It's fitting that my last blurb for the Glow is "about" (yes, using that word loosely here) a record I already reviewed for the Glow because, like, at a certain point aren't we all just doomed to repeat ourselves? They say history does it, and aren't we the ones writing it? I'm 33. I'm starting to settle in my ways, no doubt: neck-deep in the solidification phase and probably just another Kanye West release away from petrification. I am crossing that threshold point where one finds their identity—or it finds them. Growth still happens, and new challenges and struggles pour over you like a storm, weathering and eroding you, whereas new blessings (my third child is nigh) radiate upon you and you bask in them until your skin is flaking off. These things interact with the core of you, they speak to it and teach it and fuel it—but they can't change it. They only seek to expose it more.

I have to talk about this record indirectly because I said pretty much every direct thing I wanted to say about it in my review. Well, except for the way "Sleep Sound" somehow manages the paradox of seamless contrast and pliant derivation in its segue to "See Saw," a fact that was pointed out in the comments section of the review by dear reader Caleb. It's a transition like beatitude, the persistence or survival of an idea through modest variance. Doomed to repeat, blessed to repeat, to manifest anew what's just an altered version of the old, since—like the Good Book says—there's nothing new under the sun.

At this point you're begging me to say something, fucking anything, about the music here. Sorry, I can barely help myself: these are the things I think about, the things I feel, when I listen to *In Colour* (2015) the collection of music. These are the parts of myself that this music reflects back to me. If that sounds horribly insular and self-absorbed, know that I'm equally eager to hear about what this music reflects back to you, readers, just as I was to be reminded by Caleb about "Sleep Sound"/"See Saw." For this is the perfect type of music to evaluate as we will and then compare, thus exposing ourselves in the process. Magnanimously, Jamie xx gives us canvases that are wide, impressionistic, non-deterministic, largely free of built-in associations, aching with a very pure sort of inspiration, a very open absence of an overriding thought, a very warm invitation for our spirits to step in, to mingle, to dance into the night, and in the dawn to talk about who we are. We let our clothes lay on the floor, and we could let them lay there forever.

"Gosh" and "Hold Tight" stumble briefly towards their identities before gripping onto them, settling into their grooves, and what are grooves but musical metaphors for finding beauty in life's grind (and/or about sex)? And upon those grinds these tracks impose and layer elements that elevate, carrying higher forms in the cars above the rumble of the tracks, melodic and harmonic ideas that feel born from a train of thought with a perpetual motion engine, gliding on through a wasteland it can barely see. Its undying momentum transforms its perception into an approximation of contentment and sometimes even bliss, even as it runs on a track that runs round a barren world (yes, I know you've seen this movie, but at least it's not Tarkovsky). In its best moments *In Colour* vividly illustrates how gracefully taut the tension, how sophisticated the symbiosis between entelechy and evolution. The more things change the more they stay the same, right, to put it crudely. It's a theme I'm well familiar with; I wrote a play in school about it. Now, a dozen-plus years later, here's my epilogue. If I ever take a bow, it'll be to the celestial dolphin splash 'n' twirl of "The Rest is Noise."

As we talk about momentum through wastelands, I recall Kaylen Hann's excellent Unison blurb for *You're Dead!* (2014) last year, where she framed Flying Lotus's portrait of mortality in terms of velocity and acceleration. Let me tell you, having kids, I am now very fucking aware of the speed of my own mortality, and life is a highway in every way except the way Sheryl Crow meant it.

For lack of circulation my foot is dead-lead on the pedal; the signs become indecipherable, momentary blobs of green and yellow. The radio is playing, non-stop hits, "the '80s, '90s, and Today," whatever "Today" is. In the back my kids are crying in their car seats, then

fighting over the DS, then sullen teenagers on their phones, and…
silent. I glance over my shoulder; their seats are empty. I look ahead
and now everything's whipping by so fast the texture of it is incoher-
ent, like racing on the original Playstation. The radio's static. I slump
over the wheel. I dream my vehicle has wings. No, rockets. No, a
warp engine. We're all in it, we all share this intergalactic lifeboat on
its way to a massive, massless whirlpool. You're there, too. But the
boat's gone. As you speed through space towards a destination you're
not sure you want to reach, the stars streak, refracted and smudged
into a vortex of color. Soon there is no external relation to judge
one's movement or place by. Are you even moving now, really? Does
it matter? In this *Colour* your extraneous self is stripped away. There's
such a glow. And the glow is from what's left of you…a gleaming,
dying spark, wherein all emotion and thought are blurred into one
ambivalent charge. Young Thug's here, too, but ignore that for the
moment. A moment which, by the way, might be eternal, if time really can slow down to a virtual stop. And the secret you discover now
is this: the music of the spheres is the music of being. Music speaks
to that music, as deep cries out to deep (heyo, Bible reference #2). So
I guess I truly am doomed/destined to repeat myself, again and again
and again: music is a blessing. Be blessed.

CONTRIBUTORS

BRENT ABLES is a writer and editor living in Ontario with his dog.

MARK ABRAHAM is a historian, teacher, editor, coder, and project manager based in Toronto, Ontario.

CHRISTOPHER ALEXANDER is a graduate of The Evergreen State College and is plotting his comeback in Chicago, IL. He records under the name C Alexander.

CONRAD AMENTA's work also appeared in *Motherboard*, *Kill Screen*, *Logic*, *The Mark*, and a couple of dry health policy journals. He lives in Oakland.

ALAN BABAN is a writer and psychiatrist based in London.

COREY BEASLEY has written for the *Village Voice*, *Mashable*, *Paste*, *Consequence of Sound*, *the Oyster Review*, and elsewhere. He lives in Richmond, VA, where he's working on a novel.

CHET BETZ (commonly Chad, legally Charles) is based in Columbus, OH. He's written for *Kill Screen* and *Paste* and is currently writing a novel he'll never finish.

ADAM DOWNER is a writer and musician based in Brooklyn,

New York. He regrets that cokemachineglow shuttered before he was able to integrate Kpop into its usual coverage.

JOEL ELLIOTT is a filmmaker and documentary researcher based in Toronto.

JESSICA FAULDS is a renter in Vancouver, BC. She makes music under the name Expansion Club.

DAVID GOLDSTEIN is an attorney and dad living in New York City's Lower East Side. When he isn't cursing out the New York Mets, you can find him producing and co-hosting a variety of podcasts for Osiris Media.

KAYLEN HANN is a copywriter based in Brooklyn.

CALUM MARSH is a writer based in Toronto. His work appears regularly in *The New York Times*.

MAURA MCANDREWS lives in Oklahoma where she writes, plays music, and teaches/does office job stuff at the University of Oklahoma. She also co-hosts the TV podcast 714 Delaware St.

COLIN MCGOWAN writes, edits, and loiters a lot of places. He lives in Chicago.

CHRIS MOLNAR is founder of Archway Editions, the literary imprint of powerHouse Books.

AARON NEWELL used to write on the internet.

ANDRE PERRY is the author of the book *Some of Us Are Very Hungry Now* (2019). He lives and works in Iowa City.

CLAYTON PURDOM is a writer and editor based in Shaker Heights, Ohio. His work has appeared in *GQ*, *Pitchfork*, *the A.V. Club*, and *Kill Screen*.

SCOTT REID is an editor and musician from Newfoundland, where he founded cokemachineglow in 2002. He currently lives in Halifax, Nova Scotia.

ERIC SAMS is the associate director of social media for *Wired*. He previously helmed social media for *GameSpot* and *IGN*. He lives in Los Angeles.

DOM SINACOLA is a writer/editor in Portland, Oregon. His work has largely appeared in *Paste Magazine*, where he served as an editor for years.

ROBIN SMITH lives in Yorkshire. He works for Huddersfield Contemporary Music Festival, runs a small tape label called don't drone alone and plays saxophone in a metal band called Lo Egin.

LINDSAY ZOLADZ has written for the *New York Times*, *Pitchfork*, *NPR*, *Vulture*, and other outlets.

ACKNOWLEDGEMENTS

Between their debut on Cokemachineglow.com and anthologizing here, Andre Perry's essays appeared in *Some of Us Are Very Hungry Now* (2019), his debut collection of essays from Two Dollar Radio.

Nothing in this book would exist without the editorial vision and steady leadership of Scott Reid.

All of the pieces in it were originally edited by the broader CMG editorial team: Mark Abraham, Chet Betz, Dom Sinacola, Aaron Newell, Corey Beasley, and Amir Karim Nezar. Additionally, I want to thank Chris Molnar at Archway Editions for reviving this project and helping get it over the finish line.

Lastly, I want to thank everyone who ever wrote for Cokemachineglow: Aaron Newell, Adam Downer, Alan Baban, Alex Weber, Allie Conti, Amir Nezar, Andre Perry, Andrew Hall, Andy Watkins, David Greenwald, Brent Ables, Brian Riewer, Bryan Bodell, Bryan Rowsell, Calum Marsh, Chet Betz, Chris Molnar, Christopher Alexander, Colin McGowan, Connor Morris, Conrad Amenta, Conrad Tao, Corey Beasley, Craig Eley, Danny Roca, David Ritter, David Abravanel, David Goldstein, Dominick Duhamel, Dom Sinacola, Drew Hinshaw, Elana Max Dahlager, Eric Krumins, Eric Sams, Evan Goldfried, Frank Stephens, Garin Pirnia, George Bass, Philip Guppy, Jack Moss, Jessica Faulds, Joe Frankland, Joel Elliott, Jonathan Wroble, Jordan Cronk, Justin Langille, Kate Steele, Kaylen Hann, Kevin Yuen, Lawrence Lui, Lindsay Zoladz, Logan Young, Marissa Muller, Mark Abraham, Marc Piccolo, Mark Karges, Matt Main, Matt Poacher, Matt Stephens, Maura McAndrew, Peter Bauer, Peter

Hepburn, Peter Holslin, P.M. Goerner, Robin Smith, Ryan Pratt, Sam Donsky, Scott Reid, Sean Ford, Skip Perry, Todd Aman, Tom Lesiczka, and Traviss Cassidy.

To see a much more representative list of CMG's greatest hits, check out our full longlist at **cokemachineglow.com**.

MORE FROM ARCHWAY EDITIONS

Ishmael Reed – *The Haunting of Lin-Manuel Miranda*
Unpublishable (edited by Chris Molnar and Etan Nechin)
Gabriel Kruis – *Acid Virga*
Erin Taylor – *Bimboland*
NDA: An Autofiction Anthology (edited by Caitlin Forst)
Mike Sacks – *Randy*
Mike Sacks – *Stinker Lets Loose*
Paul Schrader – *First Reformed*
Archways 1 (edited by Chris Molnar and Nicodemus Nicoludis)
Brantly Martin – *Highway B: Horrorfest*
Stacy Szymaszek – *Famous Hermits*
Ishmael Reed – *Life Among the Aryans*
Alice Notley – *Runes and Chords*

Archway Editions can be found at your local bookstore or ordered directly through Simon & Schuster.

Questions? Comments? Concerns? Send correspondence to:

Archway Editions
c/o powerHouse Books
220 36th St., Building #2
Brooklyn, NY
11232